THE CULT
EXPERIENCE

THE CULT EXPERIENCE

Responding to the New Religious Pluralism

J. GORDON MELTON
and ROBERT L. MOORE

The Pilgrim Press • New York

Library of Congress Cataloging in Publication Data

Melton, J. Gordon.
The cult experience.

Bibliography: p. 169
Includes index.
1. Cults—United States.   2. Conversion—Psychological
aspects.   3. United States—Religion.
4. Deprogramming—United States.   I. Moore, Robert L.
II. Title
BL2530.U6M43   1982   291'0973   82-16136
ISBN 0-8298-0619-9 (pbk.)

The Pilgrim Press, 132 West 31 Street, New York, New York 10001

FOR OUR FAMILIES

TABLE OF CONTENTS

PREFACE

Many books have been written in recent years on the topic of cults. Most of those directed to a popular audience have further contributed to the hysteria and misinformation surrounding the issue of the cult experience. They have not clarified the discussion of the topic and have in fact added to an already confused situation. This book should have been written several years ago. Although we recognized the need for such a book sometime ago, we assumed someone else would surely write it. When no one did we finally decided to take time away from our primary areas of academic research and writing to respond to a growing public need.

This book provides both laypersons and professionals with an overview of this important cultural and religious phenomenon. It draws on the best knowledge compiled by researchers in several fields to analyze the problems created by the contemporary encounter of society and the church with the many alternative religious forms now beckoning, especially to our youth. We hope it will offer the general public—but especially church members—a way to understand the complex issues lying behind the obvious pain and confusion resulting from this encounter.

Past treatments of minority religions have all too often combined half-truths with pseudoscientific nonsense, resulting in widespread hysterical and paranoid responses. These responses led directly to a new form of religious bigotry that now enjoys much support not just in our society but also around the world.

This book combines two overriding concerns. First, we have seen on a regular basis the pain and anguish of a family split when a member joins a different religious group. Second, we are aware of the attempts by anti-cult groups to use this pain and anguish in their attacks on the alternative religions in general. These attacks have violated the personal and civil liberties of hundreds of individuals. Furthermore, the bigotry that has resulted has found tacit support among many religious and political leaders. Thus, we write, on the one hand, to offer support to individuals caught in the grip of family conflict related to religious differences. At the same time we hope to counter the new religious bigotry.

In writing this book we benefited from the assistance of many people on every side of the issue who graciously gave their time and shared their experiences. In addition, our scholarly colleagues went out of their way to keep us apprised of research data and new information; Professors Rodney Stark of the University of Washington, Eileen Barker of the London School of Economics, and Melvin Prosen of the Rush Medical College were particularly helpful. Prof. Elizabeth Payne Moore edited several of the chapters. No one deserves more gratitude than Marlene V. Woodson, who deciphered our handwriting and turned pages of rough drafts into a cleanly typed manuscript. The Chicago Theological Seminary has given us generous assistance throughout the project. Finally, we appreciate the encouragement of those colleagues who,’ when hearing of our intention to write this book, smiled and said, "It's about time."

J. Gordon Melton
Robert L. Moore

Chicago, Illinois

THE CULT
EXPERIENCE

INTRODUCTION

The American religious landscape changed during the 1960s and 1970s. Ministers, seminary professors, and religious scholars noticed it, and so did lay people. Suddenly, all of us began to feel the presence of a number of seemingly alien religions operating in our neighborhoods. Even if we did not see them, we read about gurus coming from the East and Californians getting turned on to Zen. We heard cries of political revolution turn into testimonies of conversion to unconventional religious ideals.

Those attempting to interpret this change proposed two main models. First, a number of religious scholars—especially a group associated with the Center for the Study of Contemporary Religious Movements at the Graduate Theological Union in Berkeley, California—began to talk about a "new religious consciousness." As one of their number put it, "A new self-awareness and spiritual sensitivity are finding expression in the lives of large numbers of people, especially among the young."[1] They saw, particularly in the more visible Asian religions, a key indicator of this change. Thus, the term new religions entered the world of religious conversation.

A second model, germinating from the old model of "cults," grew more out of public reaction and a sense of threat over the visible presence of so many different kinds of religions, some barely recognizable as religion by traditional standards. From this perspective, cults are seen as basically alien religions that are incompatible with the dominant cultural milieu. Some people have always been wary of cults, but a large anti-cult movement appeared during the 1970s that went beyond mere polemics to organize public and legislative opinion against these "alien" bodies.

According to anti-cultists, the alternative religions bring both a new and a sinister influence into American culture. They seem different partly because they are perceived as using sophisticated techniques of coercive behavior to recruit and hold members. These groups, anti-cultists assert, attempt to destroy the family unit, deceive the public and their own members, and engage in violent and illegal activities.

Both models agree in their perception of newness, but neither directly addresses the phenomenon itself. The new religions model, developed as it was during the height of the religious revival of the early 1970s, drew heavily on the spirit of the Aquarian age. (The idea of the coming of a new age was itself a major tenet of the revival.) Those espousing this model took Berkeley and the nearby communities of the Bay area as their major laboratory, choosing therefore one place where the Asian phase of religious exuberance was strongest. In focusing so extensively on the Berkeley phase of the revival, this model tended to ignore the history behind the revival and the prior revivals on which this one was built.

Now, almost a decade later, when the revivalistic fires have largely burned over, the continuity of this revival with the century-long processes of American—even Western—religious history can be more easily discerned. We hope people can assess these "new" religious groups with a more detached perspective. Obviously, Asian religions have been on the American scene for more than a hundred years. Interestingly, they did not grow significantly in numbers as a result of the general religious fervor of the early 1970s. The many new organizations that appeared still count their members in the thousands, if not the hundreds. In a country of 220 million they

4

remain a small percentage of the population from which to project trends. Furthermore, the group that has possibly touched the most people, the Transcendental Meditation movement, is more noteworthy for the number of ex-meditators it has spawned than for its current membership.

Most important, the particular world view or the "new" religious consciousness of these movements is by no means demonstrably new. In fact, it carries on the monistic spirituality of the older metaphysical and occult community typical of the largest segment of alternative religion in America during this century.[2] Thus, we see in the revival not the emergence of a new consciousness so much as the adoption of the old consciousness of American alternative religion by a small portion of the young adult population.

The question of the "new" religions fascinates the scholarly community, but the more pressing concern for religious leaders, church members, and the public at large grows out of the cult model. It is primarily this model that this book counters. Proponents of this model wish not merely to sell a perspective, but to encourage us to join them in a social and political effort to squelch the alternative religions. Thus, public policy is at issue as we evaluate the adequacy of the anti-cult model and the program it has spawned.

In making the case for the newness of the alternative religions, anti-cultists have focused on a single phenomenon: the tension between the alternative religions and society. Accordingly, they point to the flow of people who have joined but then, becoming disillusioned, left the religious groups. In other words, anti-cultists uncritically accept the reports of a small number of ex-members who have left groups in bitterness or who have been through the deconversion process known as deprogramming.

In making their case anti-cultists ignored the phenomena of alternative religion in America. Indeed, many seem unaware of it. Also, they describe as new certain psychological techniques that have been fairly common persuasive methodologies since the days of Charles Finney's pre–Civil War activity, if not the time of Jonathan Edwards.[3]

Alternative religions, indeed all religions in a free competitive situation, have long known and used a range of sociological and

5

psychological techniques to hold members. Having eschewed the political coercion of a state church, religions naturally use various socialization techniques to build membership into a community of like-minded people. Even mainline churches enjoying the approval and support of society at large typically rely on methods learned in group dynamics to keep their "sheep" from straying. Alternative religions, however, live in tension with society. They grow primarily by taking in converts, individuals who in turn commonly express societal conflict in familial situations.

The conflict between society and religious group can lead to violence. Faced with visible and vocal enemies, groups often respond with heightened rhetoric. Not uncommonly, they call down supernatural invectives against perceived enemies, take recourse in court, and adapt their public lives to counter the attack. Highly committed but usually isolated individuals will on occasion take the situation into their own hands and (even in defiance of the group) commit acts of violence. A historical list of such acts of violence includes mob beatings, the murder of Joseph Smith, the Mountain Meadows massacre, the bombing of Krishna Venta's headquarters, and the burning of convents and monasteries in the mid-19th century.

Neither the new religions model nor the cult model adequately explains the new situation of American religion or the role of diverse alternative religions now so obviously present in urban America. We seek to offer a more precise evaluation of this period of change and transition in American religious life.

We hope to help remove the aura of fear and threat surrounding the discussion of different religions. Few people have taken the time to examine closely the alternative religious traditions that the cults espouse. Truly, they represent alternatives to traditional Christianity, and their seemingly odd behavioral patterns become comprehensible only after one understands the world views that inform the faiths motivating their behavior.

There is something new—radically new—about the alternative religions. The newness is not to be found in the religions themselves, but in the new situation in which we who are adherents of the more established and traditional Western faiths find ourselves. Not since

6

the early days of Christianity have we had to face such a massive range of competing religions and do it without the political clout or the will to suppress them.

THE REAL ISSUE: THE NEW PLURALISM

The novelty with which scholars and the lay public now struggle is, in fact, a new, radical religious pluralism that has been growing for a century. Since World War II it has exploded and begun to intrude on traditional religious power structures.

Paralleling the growth of alternative religions is the increased fragmentation of the Christian church in the United States. One can get a hint of this fragmentation by consulting figures in the *Yearbook of American and Canadian Churches*,[4] which gives statistics for more than two hundred American church bodies. For every church listed there, three others exist. More than 800 Christian denominations currently dot the scene, and by no means are the unlisted 600 merely small, insignificant schisms. They include, for example, the million-and-a-half-member Baptist Bible Fellowship and other large separatist fundamentalist organizations.

This is only the beginning. More than 600 unconventional alternative religious bodies also compete for members. Not only has the whole spectrum of Asian religions—Hinduism, Buddhism, Jainism, Shinto, and Confucianism—arrived, but Islam has blossomed and Orthodox Judaism in the form of Hasidism is also experiencing a rebirth. To these we must add metaphysical, psychic, occult, and magical groups, as well as the Latter-Day Saints and other communalists. The list staggers the imagination.

What makes the situation new? America has experienced pluralism, even at the interfaith level, throughout the century. If the unconventional and alternative religions are neither new nor newly present in the culture (a la cult theory), what is left? We suggest four factors.

1. Recognition of the new pluralism. Certainly, *recognition* of the group has been important. One might say with some legitimacy

7

that the authentically novel thing about the alternative religions is that a group of scholars only recently discovered their presence in American society. During the late sixties and early seventies certain religious scholars noticed a number of alternative religions operating in northern California. Shortly thereafter alert scholars in other parts of the country and in Canada discovered similar groups in their own environs. Primarily motivated by a social scientific concern with the hippie and counterculture phenomenon of the 1960s, these scholars inadvertently came to dominate a field of religious inquiry that up to then had been confined to a modest group of conservative Christian researchers.

Media attention followed scholarly recognition. Bizarre religious phenomena have always made good copy for newspaper and magazine articles. Profiles of aggressive alternative religious groups filled countless columns of print, bringing home to the American public that these groups had spilled over from the fruit and nut fields of California.

The anti-cult movement did much to publicize the alternative religions. In fact, much of the media attention paid to the cults directly sprang from the warlike situation between alternative religions and anti-cultists. That war left many scars and casualties, yet it also spread public awareness of alternative religions. Even in their often hostile attacks, the press nevertheless heightened public interest in these groups.

2. *Penetration of culture by alternative faiths.* Numerically, the alternative religions do not command the numbers commonly ascribed to them. One scholar has argued that there were actually more Buddhists in America in the 1860s than today,[5] and the various national polls have noted no increase in "cult" membership in the last decade. The more successful groups have less than 10,000 members, whereas most number less than a thousand. Nevertheless, audiences are surprised to learn that the Unification Church, for example, has less than 5,000 members in the United States, because the press often gives the impression of far larger numbers. The image of the alternative religions growing by leaps and bounds and heading toward a dominant position in the religious landscape of the future

8

is plainly false. The change occasioned by alternative religions has not been due to numbers, but to the different composition of their membership.

Before World War II the majority of members in unconventional religions, particularly the historic Eastern ones, could be found in ethnic communities. They were typically Japanese-Americans or Chinese-Americans or were intellectuals like members of the Washington Friends of Buddhism. Sometimes outsiders joined, but neither type of group was particularly evangelical or aggressive.

World War II and its aftermath began to alter the situation. Some soldiers stationed as occupation forces in Japan, for example, discovered Buddhism and brought it home with them. In fact, the first significant wave of a popular non-Christian religion in the United States was the Beat Zen movement of the 1950s. In addition, President Lyndon Johnson repealed the Oriental Exclusion Acts in 1965, opening the doors for large-scale immigration from India, Hong Kong, and Japan. Among these newcomers were a number of religious leaders who sought to spread the gospel of their religion in the West, just as American Christians had spread Christianity in the Orient a century before. They found a fertile mission field.

Many of the Hindu and the Buddhist missionaries had come to speak to the immigrant communities of their own compatriots. As a matter of fact, the ethnic communities provided a well-established base from which many of the religious leaders could operate. In addition to rekindling fervor in their own communities, these religious leaders formed small study groups in academic communities for devotees of the Buddha's philosophy; for example, and they began to teach a whole generation about world religions.

The "new" Eastern missions had found a foothold by the late sixties and were prepared to reap the benefits when the wave of religious enthusiasm swept the nation in the early 1970s. That revival, typified most dramatically by the rise of the Jesus People and the consequent disruption of many mainline churches by the charismatic movement, witnessed the growth of many oriental faiths. This time the pattern of growth was new, for these religions now moved out of their former ethnic confines into Middle America.

9

Thousands (but not millions) of young white adults, educated and middle class, joined; more significantly, several million—if one is to believe the surveys—took classes in meditation, yoga, and various spiritual disciplines.

No longer confined to ethnic, lower-class, or intellectual ghettos, the alternative religions had found a new audience. They moved into Middle America and claimed members who had no intention of living on the fringe of society. Furthermore, the missionaries did not see themselves as ministering to social dropouts. Having come from a situation in which they were the dominant religion, they had every expectation of eventually becoming a respected part of this society.

The result of their decade and a half of work is not impressive in terms of sheer numbers. For every member an alternative religion now claims, ten have come and gone. But enough have remained to create a settled space in society. They are here to stay.

3. *Urbanization and mobility.* Certain social forces—especially urbanization and intensified geographical mobility—contributed to the growth of alternative religions in the 1960s and 1970s. These alternative religions are a distinctly urban phenomenon. Few have anything more than an occasional retreat center outside a major urban complex. Also, their growth in significant numbers did not come until after 1920, by which time the United States had become a predominantly urban society. Overwhelmingly, the alternative religions still in existence were organized after 1950; many grew up in the space formerly occupied by now-defunct parent bodies.

To religious bodies seeking to establish themselves the new urban complex offered two great assets: a pool of prospective members and anonymity. The sheer number of people in an average urban center guarantees a small group the freedom to assemble around almost any theological or programmatic structure. Leaders of alternative religions know this, and the growth of such religions reflects a distinctly urban pattern, usually beginning on the East or the West Coast. The city also provides the anonymity that allows a fragile, unconventional religion to grow and mature without the

10

immediate negative social pressure that could interfere with its development.

Finally, the increased mobility of American society affords alternative groups a larger pool of less-rooted individuals to attract to membership. To begin with, those who move from rural areas are likely to relocate in an urban complex. Also, Stark, Bainbridge, and Doyle have noted that these groups grow best on grounds where traditional churches are weakest—in the western states.[6] Not only do Americans now move every five years, but many who move long distances migrate to western United States. Thus, one is not surprised to find most alternative bodies in western cities.

4. Immigration. The tendency is to ignore immigration's role in the development of the diversity so radically present in American society. From the beginning, the majority of American religions have been imports, first from England, then from the rest of Europe. Tension mounted each time the pattern changed. One remembers the significant protest when immigrants from predominantly Roman Catholic countries began to arrive. Their growing presence changed the economic and political makeup of America and spawned an anti-Catholic (read "anti-cult") movement, complete with violence and horror stories told by ex-Catholics.

After World War II—and especially after 1965—patterns of immigration began to change. Asians became prominent in the list of new Americans. They were joined by a large number of Middle Eastern immigrants, who were responsible for the spread of Islam in the United States. Both groups sought to burst out of the ethnic enclaves in which they had been confined. Now one finds them quietly at work, building for themselves new temples and a new future as their members become established in American society.

THE NEW SITUATION

Alternative religions claim a small percentage of the American religious community; nevertheless, they signal a transition away from Christian hegemony to a radical pluralism. Alternative groups

11

are not ephemeral phenomena that, like the Spiritualists or Theosophists of former generations, can be written off as shallow imitations of religion and the temporary homes of a few of society's misfits and rejects. Spiritualism and Theosophy are still alive and are more vigorous than ever; they have been joined by others, which together make up a social movement too significant to dismiss and too vast to destroy.

These alternatives, along with the more established religions, are creating in the United States—indeed in all Western society—a microcosm of world religion. In almost every American urban complex one can find the full range of Middle Eastern and Asian religions, with numerous variations. They are slowly transforming the religious landscape. This transformation has already taken place in those urban communities where Sikh restaurants, Buddhist temples, and yoga centers dot street corners. In the schools the children of Pagans, Parsis, and psychics sit beside those of Jews and the many Christian denominations. Within the older churches the clergy must minister to families split by religious differences.

The new religious scene creates a new situation for the church. As the still-dominant religious body in Western culture, the church has a peculiar leadership role. We have the task of interpreting for the culture the change it is experiencing and of using creatively that tension which the changing situation is forcing on society. We also have the task of ministering to families and individuals caught in the wake of this significant cultural transition.

On both fronts a tremendous ignorance about life in alternative religious groups, even in various other fairly mainline Christian denominations, has been noted among the general populace. This ignorance has been augmented by those who wish to use public debate on the issue to promote a crusade against the cults. To counter advances by alternative groups, anti-cultists often focus on half-truths and call for simplistic and blunt action against the alternative religions. In so doing they remain unaware of the consequences of their actions for all religions, including their own. By creating a crusade against the "strange" and "alien" groups, anti-cultists have succeeded in oversimplifying the issues and distorting the realities that lie in different religions.

By focusing on the cult experience, we hope to remove the mystery and misunderstandings that have shrouded alternative religions. Although such a task is not easy, a decade of involvement in the life of alternative religions has convinced us that simple pictures invariably distort any religion. Alternative religions are neither sinister forces nor the new wave of religious consciousness for 'the future. Rather, they are social and religious groups made up of individuals who, like other religious devotees, often fail to live up to their own religious ideals. They practice religions that seem strange and exotic only because most people remain ignorant of other religious traditions and the rich diversity and heritage of the Western Christian tradition.

The Cult Experience addresses this task. As ministers during the 1970s, both of us were forced into the tense interface between the alternative religions and the mainstream culture, one as the director of a research institute studying minority religions, the other as a pastoral counselor. Because we were called on to mediate family conflict caused by a member joining a different religion, we became directly aware of the pain such situations often engender. On a more public level, we observed the controversy raised when anti-cult groups attempted to gain public support for action against the alternative religions.

In this book we present the broad context of these alternative religions, concentrating on religious groups that have become especially prominent through their penetration of white middle-class culture during the 1970s and describing these groups in the context of America's growing religious pluralism. Also, we discuss the individuals who converted to alternative religions, focusing on why they joined and the nature of their conversion, and examine the cult controversies of the seventies. We offer our appraisal of the contemporary anti-cult movement based partially on an examination of prior waves of antireligious bigotry.

Finally, we address ourselves to those who, like us, have been impacted by the religious controversy. In so doing, we offer an agenda for action by the church in the face of this new pluralism. As part of this discussion, we offer guidelines for helping families who are split by religious differences.

13

CHAPTER 1

Understanding Cults

What is a cult? What makes a Moonie a cultist? What specifically do Scientologists, Hare Krishnas, and the Children of God have in common? It is certainly not a common belief or a common set of religious practices. These four groups are as different as one could imagine, religiously speaking. Then what is it? A cult is a cult. That is to say, cults are religions that espouse an alien belief system that deviates strongly from the traditional faiths with which most people have grown up.

Cults deviate. They are different. Members stand on street corners and dance and chant. They claim allegiance to an oriental teacher or guru. They practice strange exercises, like Kundalini Yoga; they speak a strange language about ascended masters and attend secret rituals and meetings from which outsiders are barred. Possibly most important, they really believe and orient their lives around their religion, and many actively seek new converts. They do not follow what is in many homes a conventional Sunday morning religion.

That cults deviate from standard-brand religion and familiar church life give them a second shared trait: They are feared and disliked. On both a rational level and an emotional level they are little understood. The majority of people view them as threats, believing that they subvert personal values, tear apart families, and rend the social fabric.

The fear evoked by the term cult was strongly reinforced by the incident that took place in Jonestown, Guyana in 1978. Powerful descriptions of the death scene, photographs of the bodies, and subsequent stories of harsh treatment of children and violent actions reinforced the emotional charge the term cult connotes.

Both before and after Jonestown a flood of books on cults attempted to fill the void in public knowledge about these new groups. Most of these volumes, however, were written by individuals with limited knowledge of the groups about which they chose to speak so authoritatively. Hence, more attention was given to marshaling a rationale for opposing the cults in every way than to assisting readers, particularly those closest to the problems raised by the cults, to understand what the cults are doing. Families who have a relative—son or daughter—join a strange religion need information that will help them confront the situation rather than cause them to experience further emotional pressures that could push them into near hysteria.

To begin to understand the cults and the tension they have created in American life, the derogatory and pejorative connotations the word cult has must be put aside for a time and these groups examined in the broader context of American religion in general. Initially, such a change in viewing these strange groups may be difficult, but it can be rewarding and open doors of understanding by which a minority religion that has been encountered directly can be evaluated.

WHAT IS A CULT?

Traditionally, social scientists saw cults as small religious groups that shared a specific set of characteristics: First, these groups deviated widely from the dominant faith of the society in which they existed. Second, they were led by one person, a charismatic leader, who knew personally and was accessible to each member and whom each member saw as the embodiment of some cosmic force or transmitter of supernatural reality. Such a leader could be a messiah figure, a prophet, a Spiritualist medium, or a healer. Father Divine, Mother Ann Lee, and Mary Baker Eddy all filled one of these roles. Third, the membership was transient, and the group was destined to rise and fall during a single generation, usually breaking up after the leader's death.

Initially, researchers formed this rather specific and neat definition by examining the classic cults—Spiritualism, Theosophy, Father Divine's Peace Mission, and Christian Science. Later researchers have reexamined the early work and all but destroyed the classic definition. They found a lack of historical perspective on the part of those who formulated the original definition. Cults do not die after their leaders' death. All the classic cults, some older than a century, still survive; most are more vigorous today than when they were first studied.[1]

What, in fact, the early researchers of cults were describing was first-generation religion. In the first generation new religions tend to be built around a single person, who starts or creates the new faith because he or she has had a new insight, a strong religious experience, a vision, a revelation, or a strong sense of mission. New groups are usually small and grow through personal contact and the charismatic magnetism of the leader(s). During the first generation, members are most radical in their behavior, strongest in their attachment to the faith (there is no stronger member of any group than a recent convert), and most changeable, as feedback on the group seeps in from the culture and group processes are routinized.

Such insights have led social scientists to reevaluate their definitions of a cult. They now understand it as an alternative religion; that is to say, a *cult is a religious group that presents a distinctly alternative pattern for doing religion and adhering to a faith perspective than that dominant in the culture.* What is a cult is relative to the culture, thus one understands the attempts in some cultures to curb the influence of such cults as the Methodists, the Presbyterians, the Episcopalians, and the Roman Catholics because they deviate so widely from established Hindu, Buddhist, and Islamic religion.

Social scientists were not the only ones to write about cults. Most books on cults were written by evangelical Christians. For them, cults were religions with special revelations that set aside the biblical orthodoxy. The revelation might supplement the Bible, like the Book of Mormon, or be entirely distinct, such as the Theosophical writings of Helena P. Blavatsky and Annie Besant. In any case, they see cults as antibiblical and out to deceive the public with a false gospel.[2]

Both social scientists, in their attachment to deviation as a basic notion to understand cults, and evangelical Christians, in their polemic concern to show how cults differ from their particular faith, have been obstacles to an evaluation of the cults in themselves as positive elements in the religious environment of America.

RELIGIOUS ALTERNATIVES IN AMERICA

The predominant American religions (churches) emerged within a set of denominational families that share a common set of beliefs, a similar history, and a concern for certain practices (worship, ethics, etc.). Most of us are familiar with these church families and were likely raised in one of them. They go by names like Presbyterian, Methodist, Baptist, Catholic, Adventist, and Lutheran. There are about twenty distinct Lutheran denominations, although to an outsider each denomination would be recognizably Lutheran. The eight different families of the mainline churches include between 800 and 900 different denominations.[3]

Beyond these 900 denominations are more than 600 churches and religious bodies that do not share the Western Christian heritage or, at the very least, differ from it at several important points.[4] Like the 900 denominations, however, these groups emerged within a set of families that share a common set of beliefs, a similar history, and a concern to perpetuate certain religious practices. The 600 alternative bodies do not share the mainline Western Christian heritage—although some draw strongly on it—but represent innova-

18

tions in Western religion or the importation of oriental and Middle Eastern religion into the free religious environment of twentieth-century America. In the North America of the 1980s a microcosm of the world's religious mosaic can be found, especially in the urban areas. Almost any religion that can be found anywhere in the world can now be found in America.

Even though 600 alternative groups can be found, no one should infer that 600 distinct religions are present. For the alternative religions can be grouped into the same kind of religious families as mainline churches. At least eight families of alternative religions can be distinguished:

1. The *Latter-Day Saints,* or Mormons, grew out of the work of Joseph Smith, who claimed to have received a revelation now preserved as the Book of Mormon and other writings. Some 20 different bodies grew out of Smith's impetus.[5]

2. Communalists have dotted the American landscape throughout history, claiming a life based on mutual sharing of the efforts of production and common decisions about the rate of consumption. About 40 religious groups have adopted communal patterns.

3. The *metaphysicians,* developed from the thought and direction of Phineas Parkhurst Quimby, deny the metaphysical reality of evil and take as their mission the attainment of health, wealth, and/or happiness. Different groups adopt one or two of these goals as their standard. Within the metaphysical family Christian Science is primarily interested in the demonstration of healing and health. Metaphysical groups number 35.[6]

4. The *psychic-spiritualist groups* are built around the regular manifestation of psychic activity—most important, contact with the spirit world through mediums. They live off the findings of parapsychology and seek regularly to demonstrate the reality of the paranormal universe.[7]

19

5. *Ancient Wisdom schools* supply members with teachings they claim come from an ancient source (Egyptian, Atlantean, etc.). This wisdom is occult (hidden from the masses) and is offered only to aspiring students.

6. *Magical groups* practice magic, the art of causing change in the universe using occult cosmic powers by an act of the will. Persons who practice magic adopt such names as ceremonial magician, Witch, or Pagan.[8]

7. *Eastern religions* derive from Hinduism, Buddhism, and the many other faiths of India, Japan, China, and Southeast Asia.

8. *The Middle Eastern faiths* of Judaism and Islam have given rise to many new groups, a number of which have a distinctly mystical stance (Hasidism and Sufism).

The so-called cults—the alternative religions that made such an impact on American religion in the past two decades—come from all eight families. Most of them are imports from India and Japan, which have replaced Europe as the principal source of "new" religious organizations. Many of the new religious groups are comprised almost totally of first-generation Asian-American immigrants. With the flood of new immigrants that came to America after the removal of immigration restrictions in the 1960s came the missionaries of Asian faiths, who directed their attention to the conversion of the American public, rather than serving the religious communities being established by the immigrants.

The movement of Asian religion into the West during the past two decades remarkably resembles the movement of Christian missions into Africa and the Orient in the last century. After the Civil War, Christianity swept into Africa and the East, claiming converts. The initial response—although missions rarely claim more than a minority of the population—was a hearty "Yankee go home," especially in Asia. But missions persisted and brought into Asia and Africa the denominational chaos of the West. Once entrenched halfway around the world, Western Christian churches found cause to splinter further and create new church groups peculiar to India or China or Japan.

So the alternative faiths have settled in America. Although still a small percentage of the population, they have aroused the ire of many who would just as soon see them go away. The new religions have continued the great tradition of schism and splintering. The Latter-Day Saints are now divided into at least 20 separate organizations and the Spiritualists, into more than 100. Even the newer groups have begun. For example, the Siddha Yoga Dham, headed by Swami Muktananda, has spawned two schismatic groups formed by students: the Shree Gurudev Rudrananda Yoga Ashram, formed by Swami Rudrananda, and the Free Primitive Church of Divine Communion, headed by Bubba Free John (Franklin Jones).

One should not overlook the fact that a few of the religions that have appeared as part of the religious innovation do represent genuinely new religious gestalts and revelations to emerging religious leaders who gather followers based on their acceptance of the new perspective. Sometimes it is easier to trace a certain leader's development by following the thought of a parent group in a new direction. Thus, it is clear to see how Paul Twitchell developed Eckankar almost entirely from the Ruhani Satsang, of which he was a member for many years. But such groups as the Church of Scientology, the Holy Order of MANS, and the Church of the Tree of Life show little organizational or theological continuity with any groups that preceded them. They do, however, draw heavily on the storehouse of traditional religious ideas that their leaders have put together in distinct ways.

The recent proliferation of alternative religions in the West parallels the emergence of the many independent movements in Africa as the colonial era ended. They are creating in Africa the same extremely pluralistic religious setting.[9] Only in a few places in the world does one religion still reign with supreme hegemony. Across the Middle East new alternatives are springing up, one example coming from the ancient faith of Islam. Iran's Khomeini has spearheaded the resurgence of conservative Islamic beliefs and practices, and true to the pattern of most new movements, his followers are primarily students and young adults. Fascination with religious cults is not limited to the United States; it is a worldwide phenomenon.

Even though the drastic diversity and great number of cults seem to present a bewildering, chaotic panorama, cults are not beyond classification; each group has its own unique characteristics. The actual number of religious options and kinds of groups in America is not that great. Each group falls into one of the eight family groups discussed above or, in a few cases, blends traits from several families. Appendix A explains how a fundamental knowledge of the various families of religions can facilitate understanding the members of different minority religions.

WHERE DO THEY COME FROM?
(A Short History of American Pluralism)

The more than 1,500 religious bodies in the United States can be traced to the "great experiment" begun by the fledgling government of the newborn United States: freedom of religion. This meant no state church, to which all the nation's citizens must belong, would be named. Most of the early colonies had their own state churches, with New England being predominantly Congregational and the colonies from New York to Georgia ascribing to the Anglican faith. The founding fathers stood to lose either way if they answered the question, "Congregational or Anglican?" for the nation as a whole. So they declined to name any religion as a national church and guaranteed that no national church would ever be established. The Constitution protected the 36 churches serving approximately 5 million Americans. It did not, however, prevent individual states from favoring a particular church. Only over a period of decades were measures similar to the First Amendment added to state constitutions. Thus, in the 1850s the state church of Utah was Mormon. Finally, the Fourteenth Amendment brought an end to the practice of designating state churches.

It is hard to know if anyone saw the possibility of the emergence of anything beyond variations on Protestant Christianity as a result of the First Amendment. America became a place where people could legally experiment with religious ideas. New faiths needed only the growing freedom of an increasingly pluralist climate to blossom.

That blossoming began as soon as the restless ones crossed the mountains. The pioneers had little commitment to eastern society or religion. In their new land they sought a religion that would be compatible with their new life. The frontier faith and the churches that supplied it came to prominence in a religious wave which hit the country in the first decade of the nineteenth century. Called the Second Great Awakening, the revival launched the Baptists, the Methodists, and the Cumberland Presbyterians on a period of expansion that lasted most of the century. Furthermore, the Second Great Awakening was the first of the religious revivals that still sweep the country every two or three decades. The revivals correlate with a cycle of American cultural life: Each one seems to be preceded by several years of social and political unrest and change and followed by periods of relative social tranquillity. They also seem to coincide with periods of economic depression.

With each period in which the country turns its attention to religion, there is marked growth in older churches and the birth of new religions. Leaders of traditional religions generally see the new faiths as threats, aberrations, or heresies.

In their first generation, religions tend to be strongly evangelical. With the First Amendment's stipulation of freedom of religion, many people withdrew their names from church rolls. In fact, only about 10 percent of the population remained within their churches. So proponents of all religions faced the task of reclaiming the land for God. They set about this task with a vengeance, developing an amazing variety of "new measures" to assist people in beginning the religious life. These new measures, which spoke directly to the heart and the religious affections (to use Jonathan Edwards' term), became ingrained in American frontier faith. The measures—revivals, camp meetings, insistence on immediate conversion, the mourner's bench, excited preaching—were passed from one generation to the next by precept and example. Each generation received them, altered them to their particular time and place, perfected them, and took John Wesley's, Jonathan Edwards', and Charles Finney's early statements about them and codified them. By the end of the nineteenth century, evangelists had honed conversion to a fine art.[10]

The techniques developed by Wesley, Edwards, and Finney and passed on to the revivalists of the early 20th century are still used by the evangelical churches and many first-generation alternative groups, especially those with a Christian base—the Unification Church, the Way International, the Children of God, and the Christian Foundation. These techniques are part of a whole class of persuasive methods and hence markedly resemble Madison Avenue advertising and the so-called brainwashing techniques used in prison camps in Korea and China. Of course, the techniques of religious persuasion omit the characteristic of brainwashing, i.e., they do not begin by making their prospective recruit an unwilling captive, a characteristic essential to another persuasive technique—deprogramming—discussed below.

Throughout the 19th century each new wave of religious enthusiasm saw new groups arise—Latter-Day Saints, Spiritualists, Holiness churches, and at the turn of the century the Pentecostals. Each new church attracted more young adults than members of any other age-group. Most leaders were in their late 20s and early 30s and members in their late teens and early 20s. Members also tended to be alienated from the mainstream of economic and cultural life.

In his study of the Holiness movement Carl Oblinger noted the difference between persons who joined the movement (which developed within Methodism) and later left to join a Holiness church, as opposed to those who remained Methodists.[11] Those who left were most likely to be artisans with obsolete trades, tenant and small farmers, small-town laborers forced into the new cities, and the less educated. Few of the independent Holiness leaders had college or seminary education. Thus, while all kinds of Methodists were affected by the Holiness movement, those who left to found the independent churches usually considered themselves on the fringe of both the church and the mainstream of society.

In the 1890s America took a step that eventually led to some dramatic changes in the emergence of new religions. Before 1890 most new bodies were variations on Protestant Christianity. The Methodists and the Baptists splintered. All the continental divisions of the Presbyterian, the Lutheran, and the Reformed churches came to America and subdivided further. Only a few groups stood outside the mainstream of Western Christianity: the Spiritualists, the Theosophists, and the few atheists. The Mormons and the Christian Scientists had developed a Sunday worship service with a Protestant form and biblical language that partially concealed the extent of their departures from traditional Christianity.

In 1893 a group of liberal clergy in Chicago decided the nation needed more knowledge of and exposure to the many religions around the world. In conjunction with the Columbian Exposition they organized the World's Parliament of Religions. They brought together for the first time leaders from most of the churches in America and most of the religions around the world. The conference provided the general public several weeks of lectures on Hinduism, Buddhism, Shintoism, Jainism, Islam, and the various Christian churches.

Because of the attention given them, many Asian and Indian religious leaders recognized America as fertile ground on which their faiths could grow. As a direct result of their experience they returned to their home countries and sought approval to establish their churches in America. Eventually, many came back to America as missionaries. One whose enthusiastic reception at the World Parliament of Religions led him to found a religious group here before returning home was Swami Vivekananda, who formed the Vedanta Society in 1894. Other Hindu and Buddhist groups soon began to appear in the United States.[12]

The Pentecostal revival ushered in the 20th century and was succeeded by other periods of national revival. Each revival followed the same basic pattern. Old groups experienced a time of growth and received most of the new members. New religions arose among the alienated and the disinherited and took their places alongside the old bodies. Significantly, many new bodies died out after a few years.

Non-Christian religion spread slowly. Immigration restrictions, one of the symbols of American anti-orientalism, kept out potential leaders. Thus, Hinduism and Buddhism could only grow in proximity to the early centers of Japanese and Chinese migration—

Hawaii and the West Coast. But there they grew and began to break out of the oriental ghetto. Two events smashed the ghetto gates.

Following World War II the United States stationed occupation forces in Japan. Some of the soldiers, instead of spending their off-hours touring the countryside or stopping at the local geisha house, visited Buddhist temples. After their tours of duty they stayed to take training and then returned to found Buddhist outposts across America. The second impetus to Eastern religions came in the mid-1960s, when President Lyndon Johnson lifted the immigration restrictions against Indians and Orientals. People from the East poured into the United States in ever-increasing numbers, and their ministers and priests (under such labels as swami, guru, and yogi) began to arrive. The swamis and teachers who came earlier as token leaders were eclipsed by the relatively large number of teachers who brought the wide range of Asian teaching to the United States.

Like Christianity, Hinduism and Buddhism had splintered into a multitude of theologies, groups, and organizations. Just as Methodists, Baptists, Pentecostals, and Jehovah's Witnesses presented a bewildering array of American Christian truth on the Asian and African mission fields, so Shin Buddhists, Kundalini Yogis, Hare Krishnas, and Zen meditators have brought the bewildering kaleidoscope of Asian faiths to North America.

Most of the new religions that became prominent in the 1970s actually arrived and became settled in the 1950s and 1960s. During this period their growth was sluggish. Especially during the 1960s, the nation was more interested in civil rights and peace than in "spiritual matters." As the great social crusades ended, however, people began to search for spiritual solace. Most found it in Christian forms. The neocharismatic fellowships that arose in most large Protestant denominations and Roman Catholicism claimed many more converts than the largest cult groups combined. The Assembly of God gained half again as many members in the 1970s as it had gained in the first 50 years of its existence.

A synthesis of the best data available shows the extent of the inroads new religions have made on the American scene. Of the largest "new" religions—Scientology and the Unification Church—neither seems to have much more than 5,000 and certainly no more

26

than 8,000 to 10,000 active members (i.e., persons who would consider themselves Scientologists or Unificationists). Both have less than 100 centers of operation in the United States. The Church of Scientology's claim of members in the millions seems to come from counting the multitudes that have at some point sought out or inquired about it or taken the basic personality test offered at all centers. Conversely, the Transcendental Meditation movement, which seems to have taught more than a million Americans how to meditate, claims few of these as adherents in even the most basic sense.

These figures have a double implication: In a nation of 220 million, only 5,000 to 10,000 have found their way into the largest of the new religions. Many mainline *congregations* are larger than the largest of these movements. Numerically, the new religions offer no immediate challenge to traditional religions and their membership. However, actual measurement of membership is only one category by which to judge the influence and likely future of these groups.

Although relatively few persons really join the new religions, large pockets of the population have been attracted to traditional practices of these faiths. For example, many practitioners of hatha-yoga would never think of themselves as Hindus. Millions now meditate in some form without considering themselves adherents of a new religion.

The final assessment of how many people are in fact in the new religions remains difficult. No definitive count has been made; many times the figures offered by the new groups are inflated for public relations purposes. For example, in 1978 the Church of Satan claimed more than 10,000 members. This figure included the total number who at one time, for whatever reason, sent in the $25 lifetime membership fee. Fewer than 2,000 seem to have been active at any given time (i.e., were paying their $10 per annum active fee). By 1979 membership had been drastically lowered by schism, and only three grottoes (congregations) remained active.

By the best estimate several hundred thousand persons could be considered members of alternative religions. Possibly double this number remain on the fringe as members of humanistic psychology groups, taking psychic development or practicing private meditation disciplines. A much larger number have taken Yoga, martial arts, or meditation class or have attended introductory sessions at which the various groups have attempted to recruit members.

This survey of the new religions prompts several reflections on their impact on the American religious scene. First, numerically speaking, they remain a relatively small phenomenon. Their adherents appear to be more numerous than they are because of the excessive coverage they have received in the media. Many articles, especially since Jonestown, have deliberately exaggerated cult membership figures to underline the hysteria and paint the new religions as greater threats than their actual membership would suggest.[13]

Despite their small size relative to the public or the membership of the major religious bodies, the new religions are not insignificant phenomena on the fringe of culture. The 1970s witnessed, in the emergence of the new religions, a quantum leap in religious pluralism. Although Asian faiths have been present in America throughout the twentieth century, they have been largely confined to the ethnic ghettos on the West Coast and to a few northern urban complexes. Beginning with the Beat Zen movement of the 1950s and the arrival of the many Asian teachers and religious leaders in the 1960s, the Asian faiths jumped out of the Oriental-American and the Indian-American communities into the mainstream.

In the future Eastern religions will be part of American life, as will many nonorthodox forms of Christianity and innovative forms of religion drawing on a variety of non-Christian elements. The increasing alienation of urban life, continuing disruptions of economic patterns, and higher mobility are preparing an environment in which the alternative religions can slowly continue to grow. Also, having gained a strong foothold during the 1970s, the new religions have a more secure base for expansion.

WHO JOINS THEM?

Traditionally, alternative religions have been seen as the home of the disinherited, the dispossessed, and the alienated. For example, the cargo cult of New Guinea grew up around the hopes of the native population for the rich goods of the European colonizers that arrive on airplanes. On deserted runways, natives built model airplanes from bamboo; their leaders said the gods would send bounteous gifts—cargo—as reward. American religions of the dispossessed would include Father Divine's Peace Mission, which was built from the blacks caught in the urban ghettos after World War I. Even the Peoples Temple grew by taking in the poor blacks in the California ghettos and the whites sympathetic to their needs.

But most 20th-century alternative religions do not follow the classic patterns of the "cults of the oppressed." Leaders wishing to build a community of faith have turned to the urban, middle-to-upper-middle-class young adult segment of the population. The new burst of alternative religion is an urban phenomenon. As the teachers walked off the plane from Bombay or Tokyo or left behind the farm in rural Iowa, they intended to settle in the nearest big city—New York, Chicago, Los Angeles, San Francisco, or Honolulu. Hindu teachers intended first to work in New York and then head west, stopping at Cleveland or Pittsburgh or Philadelphia on the way. Buddhists stopped first in Honolulu or California before heading east by way of Denver or Kansas City. Asian religions are still an urban phenomenon. With the exception of an occasional retreat center, most of the alternative faiths do not yet exist in the rural countryside.

Members of alternative religions tend to be among the haves rather than the have-nots. They come directly from the dominant, white, educated middle class. As a whole, those who join alternative faiths are from the upper half of the population, incomewise and educationwise. When they do join, as has been true of alternative religions in general, the new members are usually relatively young (ages 18 to 28), unmarried, and at a decision-making point in their careers. Such persons are at points where society deems it proper to make the crucial decisions about career, marriage, and faith commitments.

Many who oppose the cults have based their cases on an observation that cult members were, at the time of their joining, searching, frustrated, unsure of themselves, and overwhelmed by the pressures of life. Even though there is a certain truth to this observation, it sheds no light on the question of who joins the alternative religions. First, these factors describe a large segment of the younger generation as a whole. Hence to point out this characteristic does not answer why most young people choose more traditional patterns, such as military service, to deal with problems of adolescence and why only a few choose an alternative religion. Second, increasing observation has confirmed that members of the new religions do not show a higher rate of crisis problems and alienation than those who do not join.

One other observation: Alternative religions draw members from all the established churches and major faiths in proportion to their presence in the population. That is to say, approximately 50% of the members tend to be Protestant in background; 25%, Roman Catholic; and 25%, other. Some individual groups draw more heavily from a particular faith (for example, almost all Satanists are former Roman Catholics).

The situation is different when we come to Jewish participation. Jews make up 2% to 3% of the population, but their participation level is high in the new religions. Interestingly, with the exception of the Messianic Jewish movement—a Christian group composed almost entirely of Jews—Jewish membership is highest in non-Christian, nonevangelical groups. The one group from which many segments of the Jewish community have felt the most threat, the Unification Church, has only 5% to 6%, whereas others have as much as 25% to 30%. Compare these figures.

Religion	% of Jewish membership
Neo-Paganism	11%
Hare Krishna	12%
Sufism	15%
Zen Buddhism	25%

Further, the percentage of Jews in leadership positions is much higher.

The data seem to indicate that the worries of the Jewish community about conversionist Christian groups are largely unfounded, but the matter of why so many join alternative religions that do not proselytize does raise questions for the Jewish community, questions we do not feel qualified to answer.

Finally, it should be noted that members of the new religions are drawn largely from nonreligious and nominally religious homes. In a recent survey of Neo-Pagans, for instance, only one third reported having ever been active in a church or synagogue. Thus, alternative faiths seem to be filling a religious void in the lives of their members.[14]

WHAT IS THE APPEAL?

The final basic question about the new religions concerns their appeal. Their critics argue that they have no legitimate appeal and ascribe their growth to psychological manipulation, hypnotism, and fear. Certainly, as with all religious bodies, correlations between certain nonreligious needs and the adherence of members to a particular faith do exist. For example, many members of the larger churches maintain their membership because they grew up in these churches and know nothing else. Other churchgoers stay with their churches because of the social status of belonging to their particular Episcopal congregation or their community's first church. Still other members of mainline religions find within their congregations a number of business contacts. Motives for church affiliation are many.

Within the new religions at least five elements strongly affect membership attachments. First and foremost, a genuine spiritual immediacy exists within the nonconventional religions. The majority of the first-generation alternative religions offer their members an immediate and personal contact with a transpersonal reality. This transpersonal reality goes under many names, such as God, satori, baptism of the Holy Spirit, cosmic consciousness. Each new faith teaches the believer to contact and confront a realm of the divine beyond his or her ordinary consciousness.

The offer of an immediate experience of the divine places the new religions within the context of American revivalist traditions and helps explain their widespread success. American religion has often been a quickie affair. The frontier afforded little time and educational base for the details of theology and for the strict observance of proper church order and orthodox form. From John Wesley to Charles Finney to Dwight Moody and Billy Graham, evangelists sought ways to introduce religion into individual lives within the confines of a camp meeting or a big-city revival. In the enthusiastic atmosphere of the revivals, lives changed, and the converts filled the land with churches.

Today the new religions offer a similarly immediate experience in a wider variety of molds. Although the revivalistic practices discussed above continue, Eastern groups have added yoga, meditation techniques, and spiritual exercises. Members learn to sit in silence, to chant words (mantras), and to perform magical rituals, as well as gain knowledge from a spiritual master. Many believers—if not most—come to this new intimacy with the spiritual after having a bad experience in mainline Catholic or Protestant churches or Jewish synagogues. Having found few resources for their spiritual journey in the staid, formal atmosphere of their parents' congregations, they visit "new" religions and discover, to their surprise, much of what they are seeking.

To downplay the genuine religious atmosphere of most new religions is to miss the heart of their reality. Although many faiths teach a naive, incomplete theology and show an appalling lack of social concern, they do deal directly with the problem with which most mainline church congregations have the greatest difficulty—introducing young adults who have grown up within the congregation to the religious realities that most of the older members have long since learned to work with and integrate into their total life pattern.

Most mainline churches today are totally committed to the nurturing model of Christian education and religious development. This model, introduced years ago by Horace Bushnell, has strong points but misses many people completely. It is weakest at the points of initiating people into the life of religious experience and of assisting a community of faith in providing any space for people who have strong religious experiences to express their faith. In contrast, one might see the alternative religions as taking a more experiential, almost sink-or-swim approach. They tend to push new members into intense religious experiences and then use the reality of these experiences as the initial data for nurturing-educational programs.

Even though the dominant developmental model seems to work best for most church members, the more direct experiential approach seems to work for many people who have missed what more traditional nurturing approaches have been trying to communicate to them or who have been denied a religious life during childhood.

Second, many alternative religions offer the appeal of group intimacy. Numerous observers have noted the almost magnetic pull of group life within the new religions. An atmosphere of personal affirmation and support binds members together in a fellowship that satisfies the need for close contact with other people, so often lacking in society (and unfortunately in churches and synagogues as well).

Within the group the individual can share the inner self, find acceptance despite his or her past or status, experience forms of catharsis during moments of transition to new perspectives, and locate a place to belong—a shelter from the loneliness of the urban environment. Many young adults in today's mobile society acutely need surrogate families. After high school graduation they usually leave home and either take jobs or go "off" to school. Having lost support from family, friends, and familiar structures, they must discover or create new units of personal assistance. Dorm life, a few calls home, weekend partying, alcohol and drugs just do not accomplish this task. The young project that some day they will have careers and homes of their own, but these images of stability hold only promise, not immediate support.

At this point, especially if early religious life has failed to be supportive, some individuals find new alternatives attractive. For a few, suicide beckons. Many find new families in the form of close-knit religious fellowships, and the experience is so heartening that the name of the group hardly seems relevant.

The third drawing card of the new religions is that they offer a remythologizing of life for their converts. Remythologizing becomes particularly important within the context of the modern "cafeteria" of world views presented at the university level. Higher education provides either an overabundance of confusing and contradictory world views or the rather reductionist, humanist rationalism that has little to say about meaning, transcendence, and higher aspirations. Remythologizing is also crucial for those suffering uncertainties about a personal future. (Uncertainties are often expressed as a gap between parental expectations and an individual's more honest evaluation of his or her future.) The personal vacuum created by the university curriculum and the pressures of becoming an adult leaves many young people with a need for a religious perspective both distinct from the one they passed through in childhood and capable of making sense out of the confusion of their existence.

The critic, of course, quickly sees the weaknesses, contradictions, and unanswered questions of a cult's world view. "How could anyone believe that?" But the group supplies a basic metaphor or model by which an individual may approach life.

The fourth source of appeal of the new religions is their therapeutic dimension. Although this trait is obscured by the polemics about cults, many new religions have functioned as therapeutic communities. We discuss this further in our assessment of cult life, but here we would simply say that in this day, when the cost of psychotherapy renders it unavailable for most, the new religions attempt to satisfy the pastoral and developmental needs of their members. These needs are broad, but many of the new faiths seek to meet them by offering a safe and supportive environment in which change can be encouraged and accomplished.

Young adults often talk about getting their act together. They recognize the chaos in which they frequently and to different degrees find themselves. Yet they have rejected traditional avenues of assistance (again for a variety of reasons). The support, guidance, and discipline of the group provide the context (often in the form of a temporary relief from past pressures) in which an individual can reassess his or her life and find new directions. As shown in chapter 4, one reason for the frequent turnover in group membership is the completion of a change process: the individual no longer needs the group. He or she then leaves and continues with other career and life patterns.

The final source of appeal of the cults—definitely not to be overlooked—is that some young adults' first act of asserting their adulthood is to join a cult. The popular image of cults shows them as inhibiting or stopping maturation. This criticism is not unfounded. However, repeatedly, our interviewing and counseling with cult members has revealed a structure of assertion of independence in deciding to join a cult. The story usually begins in a "happy" family known for its lack of discord and overlay of harmony. Unfortunately, many parents deny their teenagers any avenues for the expression of hostility and anger or the communication of disagreement with parental decisions. The young may not feel ready for college, if they want to go at all. They may want to major in art, not engineering. Unable to communicate on issues that matter, they learn to keep silent. But they must grow up sometime, and growing up means severing the umbilical cord. So they drop out of school, get a job, and join a cult. Parental reaction to this series of events can determine family patterns for years to come.

CHAPTER 2

Understanding the Cultist: Snapping or Transformation?

Are typical members of contemporary cults really brainwashed zombies? That the need to address this issue is pressing is an indication of the impact of the hysterical oversimplification that has characterized too much of the recent response to the new religions. Much has been made of the sudden personality change that comes over seemingly well-behaved and "normal" young people when they enter such groups.[1] Something seems to have "snapped"— there appears to be an abrupt discontinuity between the personality before and after crossing the threshold into the life of the cult. Parents commonly find the new personality unrecognizable in many ways: uncooperative, aloof and remote emotionally, gravitating away from family values, aspirations, and life-style. The language of these persons changes, not only by the use of phrases and formulas apparently based on some esoteric religious teachings, but also by the way they relate to the phrases as they utter them. Ideas that seem incredibly garbled and irrational to the parents are treated by the young people as though they carried some magical power or significance.

When attempts are made to convince the young people that

these strange, alien ideas are unworthy of the energy and devotion they are lavishing on them, a more disturbing change occurs in the pattern of communication between the parents and their children: the aloofness increases, and the communication of the cult members becomes more evasive and less frequent and is characterized by defensiveness and sometimes duplicity and deception.

That the cultists' consciousness and behavior depart from previous patterns is a point that has been emphasized in the literature on the cults. Besides the changes noted above, cultists often dress and/or wear their hair differently—sometimes unconventionally. Books of esoteric doctrine may be offered as better alternatives to the parents' choice of scriptures, and the young people may practice some form of ritual magic and chant in strange tongues to even stranger gods and goddesses. The bizarre impression that cult members make on others—intentionally or not—is best symbolized by the assertion that there is something strange about the eyes of such persons. They are, depending on whom you talk with, hypnotic or appear to be hypnotized. They are alternatively blank, empty, glassy, robotlike, possessed, wild, secretive, and so on.

As if the above were not enough, cultists sometimes behave as if the world were in fact *sacred geography*, the locus of cosmic struggles that only the initiated can understand and deal with effectively.[2] Urgency permeates the life-world of the cultist, and she or he seems determined to engage with great commitment in activities that appear to the outsider to be at best a waste of time and at worst downright self-destructive and/or antisocial. These activities range from lengthy sessions of meditation, esoteric ritual, and the like to the aggressive evangelistic and fund-raising activities of such groups as the Unification Church and the International Society for Krishna Consciousness. Many accusations have been made concerning the alleged way in which cult members have been brainwashed—robbed of their autonomy by techniques that have been cynically designed to do away with the free will of the individual involved. Trying to get by on an inadequate diet—usually vegetarian—and prevented by the leaders from getting adequate sleep, the person reaches the state of exhaustion and becomes more vulnerable to the teachings and influences of the group.

Further, the prevalent popular interpretation goes, once this person has been deceived by the cult into thinking its activities are authentically religious, and once a cynically planned schedule of activities has brought on exhaustion, then the next step—the destruction of ties with the outside world, especially the family—can be taken. To effect this change, attempts are made to destroy the ties that bind the individual to his or her precult existence. Survival of the precult identity loses meaning for the individual, and family, friends, previous work roles, property owned before joining all come to be viewed as dangerous baggage that must be jettisoned so the new life offered by the group may come to fruition. The outside world, then, and especially anyone and anything that tempts the individual to return to the previous life, may begin to seem dangerous or demonic to the individual and may be interpreted as such by the group leaders. Now, so the popular interpretation goes, the individual is, in effect, a prisoner of the group—tricked into joining the group, subjected to techniques of brainwashing that destroy the autonomy of the individual, and then progressively isolated from the outside world while the cult takes everything and gives little in return.

A number of assumptions underlie the kind of interpretation of the personality of the cult member sketched above. The balance of this chapter seeks to offer a more complex, more accurate, and in some ways more hopeful interpretation of the cultist personality. Our interpretation differs from the above in a number of ways, and to differentiate our point of view from the above, at the outset we challenge the following assumptions:

1. *Cult members are usually coerced into joining groups against their wills or are usually deceived into joining.* Although some instances of questionable evangelistic techniques have occurred, there is little or no evidence to suggest that members have not freely chosen entry into the groups. What is clear is that entry into such groups contradicts the parents' *perceptions* of the pregroup personalities of the cultists. Our experience, however, has been that communication between these young people and their parents usually had deteriorated before their exposure to the evangelistic efforts of

the groups—and that often the facade the young people had been presenting to their parents had been deceptive for a substantial length of time. It should be clear here, however, that such deception of parents by their children is not always—even usually—a manifestation. of hostility or antagonism toward the parents. Often it masks intense feelings of shame on the part of the individuals that they have not yet been able to get it together, to find their vocations, appropriate marital partners, etc. Such deception of parents by young people often stems from a desire to spare the parents knowledge of the intensity of the pain and despondency their children may be feeling.

Some young adults have parents who give them good reason to be less than forthright about their real feelings, fears, and aspirations. Many times, while seeking to restore communication between family and cultist, we are aware immediately of why the distance has been sought by the cultist: authoritarian and intrusive styles on the part of the parents. To those with no experience in family counseling this may seem harsh. It remains, nevertheless, a common pattern in the families of "troubled" youth, and we have found that it recurs time and again in the families of cult members. Usually such parents have great difficulty recognizing the ways in which they have made developing independence a problem for their children. No "Archie Bunkers," such parents have chosen impressive, successful futures for their children—often providing in a package acceptable professions, college majors, and a list of preferred schools. One can understand that parents might feel their children would have to be brainwashed into rejecting such a promising agenda, but the children of such parents are often clearer than they are about the nature of the vicarious ambitions commonly embodied in such pressures and agendas.[3] Youth pay great prices to feel in control of their own agendas, and will—although usually with substantial guilt feelings—sacrifice early a frank and honest relationship with hopeful, ambitious but insensitive parents.

This is not to say that parents assuming their children have been brainwashed may not have observed some strange behaviors that merit concern and require responsible attention. Later in this chapter we discuss the complexities of states of transition represented in cult life that can have bizarre psychological effects. At this point, however, it is important for us to point out that an apparent radical personality change ascribed to deception and brainwashing by a cult may in reality be an attempt by the young person to be more honest about his or her real feelings, values, and commitments in the face of parental concern, pressure, and/or disapproval. In this way the movement into an alternative religious group may be a significant step toward independence from the primary family.

2. A cult member is, by virtue of cult membership, in some pathological state. How any responsible and informed professionals could come to such a conclusion is difficult to understand, unless they have already written into their assumptions, unwittingly or not, a simplistic dogmatic religious or secularist point of view. If one has a religious stance that assumes a person of another faith is either deluded by false teachers or inspired by demonic forces, then a negative interpretation of a person's involvement in a religious group that is outside the national religious consensus is guaranteed. This kind of stance is, of course, the standard fare of religious bigotry and is the same attitude that previously was applied in much the same manner to Judaism and Roman Catholicism.

The secularist assumption is more difficult to spot, particularly for those who lack sophistication with regard to the antireligious bias of much contemporary social and behavioral science. For example, sociologist James Richardson has noted that recent psychosocial interpretations of the alternative religions have been dominated by Freudian conceptions of conversion which have tended to view religious conversion as a regressive phenomenon.[4] With the exception of Erik Erikson's work and that of other recent psychoanalytic ego psychologists, the tendency has been for psychologists of a Freudian persuasion to mistake a *psychopathology* of religion for a balanced psychology of religion.[5] The key issue is whether conversion and other intense religious experiencing are seen as normal accompaniments of transition states—and particularly of the transition from adolescence to early adulthood. This is related to what we discuss below as the question of the psychodynamic

40

significance of liminal states. At this point, however, we need only note that the point of view expressed in such a book as *Snapping*[6] reflects a militantly secularist reductionistic and regressive reading of religious experience characteristic of classic Freudian and other hostile interpretations of religion in general and conversion in particular.

If an interpreter of the new religious movements adopts the assumptions about religious conversion that view conversion as pathological by definition, then converts and devotees of the alternative religions will undoubtedly be assessed by such an interpreter as manifesting psychopathology. Another tendency we have noted is for psychological clinicians who have treated a number of current or former cult members in their psychotherapeutic practices to generalize on the basis of this inadequate sample and to conclude that experience of participation in the new religions is pathogenic. That this bad logic receives any credence is incredible. Using the same approach one could sample the persons in a psychiatrist's office at any given time, give them psychological tests, and on discovering psychopathology, conclude that going to a psychiatrist's office *causes* emotional disorders!

3. If a young person manifests symptoms of psychopathology during or after involvement in an alternative religion, the group caused the disorder in a person who was without emotional difficulties before joining. This is an elaboration and expansion of the preceding assumption, which noted that participation is evidence of pathology. Now this is extended to conclude that participation caused the pathology. This assumption forms part of the foundation that, in the militant anti-cult movement, justifies the use of questionable tactics not only to remove young people from minority religions, but to legislate and otherwise act against the existence of religions that deviate from the national consensus. (This is discussed at length in chapter 3.) Richard Anthony and Thomas Robbins have discussed this quasi-scientific justification for action against minority religions in detail in their articles and papers.[7] Anthony and Robbins are social scientists who have concluded that this movement toward the "medicalization of deviant religions" constitutes not only a misuse of scientific constructs for political ends, but that involvement of the mental health establishment in the suppression of alternative religions constitutes a substantial threat to civil liberties. Further discussion of this phenomenon is presented in chapter 3 in an analysis of deprogramming and related attacks on religious liberties that are currently underway.

At this point it is important to emphasize that we are *not* suggesting that the alternative religions are free of members with emotional difficulties. We have observed emotional disturbances of varying degrees of severity among the membership of various alternative religions. Here, however, we must discipline ourselves to approach these deviant groups evenhandedly. For example, what pastor of a local church in any major denomination will not find some members with neurotic, borderline, and even frankly psychotic symptoms (if he or she possesses the clinical skills to discern them)? The answer obviously is that *all* religious groups—not just the deviant ones—have within them persons with severe emotional problems. The pastoral-care movement of recent decades has emphasized that this is where troubled persons should be! Our point is that, contrary to current popular treatments, not only is there little reason to believe that members of alternative religions are significantly more emotionally disturbed than persons in more established denominations, but claims that the groups damage persons emotionally are not substantiated by any careful quantitative empirical studies. In fact, participation in these groups often has a therapeutic impact on the personalities of group members.[8]

Let us return to the person who is a member of one of the alternative religions and does manifest frank, severe psychopathology. Most of the evidence regarding the genesis of emotional disorders places the origins of such difficulties early in the developmental process—long before any encounter with an alternative religion. Understandably, the family of an acutely disturbed cult member would prefer to project the causes of the young person's problems on another agency. This is the phenomenon of scapegoating, and however understandable it must be seen for what it is. If indeed a young person in a group is so decompensated that he or she appears to be a zombie, the chances are far better that the pathology was brought with the person to the group than that the group caused the disorder. That the so-called anti-cult groups which allegedly are so pro-family have made so little of the literature on family systems theory and family therapy should at least make parents hesitant to accept the preferred explanations of the sources of their children's difficulties. Below we discuss further the implications of family systems theory for understanding both entry into a group and possible therapeutic response.

What, then, is one to make of the observations of parents and others that the onset of symptoms in disturbed cult members coincides with entry or participation in a group? First, the sudden personality change frequently touted in popular discussions of snapping and the like is often the result of a normal transition state, not psychopathology. A maturing young adult, moving toward independence from the primary family, often manifests behaviors that are different from those to which the family is accustomed. Second—and more important here—that a young adult may manifest symptoms of psychopathology at the point at which he or she is moving toward independence is not proof that some agent external to the family matrix is responsible for the emotional disorder. On the contrary, it is a psychological commonplace that deficits in the capacity for psychosocial adaptation may not appear until the severe strain of separation from the primary family system is encountered. The psychodynamic origins of such adaptive deficits occur much earlier in the developmental process, usually—if not always—in childhood.[9]

4. *Once a person enters the sphere of influence of an alternative religion this person is forever lost to his or her family and to life outside the group.* This assumption is frequently used by deprogrammers to sell a deprogramming to distraught family members. If the person is not forcibly removed from the group, the prognosis for return to the family and what it conceives of as "ordinary" existence is deemed guarded if not hopeless. One of the saddest effects of this widely marketed assumption is the panic it tends to induce in the families of persons joining a minority religious group. Families who are led to believe this become easy prey for entre-

43

preneurs who play on their love for their children to sell the coercive tactics of deprogramming. The fact is that the majority of persons entering alternative religions leave voluntarily in a period ranging from a few months to a few years. The complex dynamics underlying this are discussed below. Here it suffices to note that it is important that families not be given hysterical misinformation concerning the prognosis for the return of their sons or daughters to life outside the groups. Families can respond more judiciously to such a crisis if they are not panicked by misinformation.

5. *All alternative religious groups are merely machines for pseudo-religious manipulation of persons who have lost their capacity to choose, and therefore participation in these groups is not to be considered an expression of an authentically religious impulse.* Contrary to popular treatments, existing research by sociological investigators indicates there is no reason to believe that entry into an alternative religion evidences any different decision-making processes than entry into other voluntary associations and activities common to a comparable population.[10] One of the fascinating and disturbing aspects of this controversy is the manner in which some theorists—arguing from a deterministic mechanistic and/or positivistic philosophical anthropology—lament the alleged loss of the capacity for free will and free choice of a person who has joined a religious group, *although their own deterministic assumptions exclude any basis for free will in the human organism.* As noted above, a militantly secularist point of view often takes a reductionistic stance toward *any* religious commitment, not just commitment to an alternative religion. It is then only a short step to considering the phenomenon of conversion to be not a legitimate religious phenomenon, but an expression of "information disease"—of snapping, in short, of a pathological failure of the human organism. We have discussed the pluralistic context of contemporary American religious life. The tendency to depreciate the religious involvements that are not in groups sanctioned by the national religious consensus is understandable, given our discussion of the anxieties occasioned by a quantum jump in religious pluralism in a culture. Nevertheless, such easy dismissal of unfamiliar religious systems and practices is

in fact a current expression of religious bigotry. In our interviews with young members of the alternative religions we have found it was often the lack of authentic religious commitment on the part of parents that led the young persons to leave the religious traditions of their families and look elsewhere for religious guidance. Rather than being an expression of some sinister factor indicative of a failure of personality and of malignant influences, the intense religiosity of late adolescents and young adults is a normal characteristic human development and an expression of their healthy religious interests and expressiveness.

The difficult fact for people to face is that they may have been such poor representatives of their own religious traditions that their children—however mistakenly—feel they must look elsewhere for practical guidance for living religiously serious lives.

Popular treatments of the cult experience have been characterized by gross oversimplification. Worse, some approaches have been based on assumptions which inevitably conclude that any conversion experience is suspect, that any intensive religious commitment entailing sacrifice and asceticism must be evidence of either brainwashing or psychopathology or both. We have argued that these assumptions must be examined carefully to discern the logical fallacies and distortions that issue from them.

We have not, however, claimed that there is no evidence of emotional disorders among persons who are or have been involved in alternative religions. On the contrary, we have suggested that although there is indeed some evidence of psychopathology, there is not sufficient empirical quantitative research evidence to justify the assumption that the incidence of disorders is significantly higher than in mainline congregations. With regard to the genesis of the emotional disorders which do exist, we have suggested that it is highly unlikely the difficulty is rooted chiefly in the groups, but rather in early childhood development and family dynamics within the primary family system.

To return to the phenomena discussed at the beginning of this chapter, we want to make it very clear that we are not denying that "strange" or "spacey" behavior may be observed among some members of alternative religions. Certainly, sudden changes in a person's behavior, diet, ideas, attitudes toward work, ethical assumptions, values, and other related aspects of his or her life may seem incomprehensible to family and friends. We argue that this type of extraordinary personality change need not be seen as characteristic solely of those group members who are suffering from psychopathology, but that such phenomena, rightly understood, may be seen to be normal expressions of ideation and behavior common to *transition states* in human personality. We now turn to the conceptual tools one needs to understand the subtlety and complexity of these phenomena.

THE CULT EXPERIENCE AND THE CONTEXT OF TRANSITION

Much has been made of the fact that the majority of persons who belong to alternative religions enter them during their early twenties. Occasionally, a commentator briefly seeks to tie entry into a cult to the difficulties of adaptation that life presents to young adults. No one, however, has grasped the extent to which the phenomena of the cult experience, to be understood properly, must be seen in the context of states of transition—particularly the transition from adolescence to young adulthood (see Figure 1). Daniel J. Levinson, in *The Seasons of a Man's Life*, calls attention to the predictable crises that normally afflict a person throughout her or his life cycle.[11] Levinson demonstrates that it is not just the "adolescent storm" and the subsequent transition to early adulthood which disturb the unfolding of a life. Rather, transitions that bring unsettling change recur periodically throughout the life cycle. Increasing realization of the importance of recurrent transition states has recently issued in the attention given to the midlife crisis and to the important adaptational problems that occur at the time of retirement. One of the most important insights that has issued from Levinson's and other similar investigations is that these crises are properly to be understood as normal developmental phenomena of human life, not as expressions of abnormal disturbance or psychopathology. This does not mean that the transition states experienced in a life pilgrimage are not disturbing and often dangerous. In a later section

46

we discuss in more detail the characteristics of consciousness and behavior that tend to appear in such states and show how the phenomena of transition are commonly misinterpreted as manifestations of a snapped or brainwashed mind or as evidence of severe psychopathology. Our task here is simply to note that entering an alternative religion usually occurs during or after the severe buffeting of early adult transition, and that in order to grasp the nature and significance of the cult experience as it relates to psychosocial issues, the experience must be seen in the context of transition state phenomena. From our point of view, this contexting is the sine qua non of responsible discussion of the personalities of members of the alternative religions. That this contexting has not already been highlighted in popular interpretations of the cult experience is largely responsible for the oversimplifications, misrepresentations, and hysteria that have commonly plagued journalistic treatments of the phenomena, particularly those of the so-called anti-cult movement. The following brief discussion lifts up the necessary conceptual tools and information one needs to understand the complexity of the psychosocial issues that are raised when this controversial topic is approached.

RESOURCES FROM CULTURAL ANTHROPOLOGY: VICTOR TURNER ON RITUAL PROCESS

Victor Turner is undoubtedly one of the most important theorists in contemporary psychosocial interpretation. His cultural anthropological approach, usually referred to as *processual symbolic analysis,* has updated the work of Van Gennep on rites of passage and has generated significant insights into the interaction of culture and personality.[12] Of value for our purposes here is the manner in which Turner's work illuminates the nature and dynamics of transition states as seen in their social context.

Following Van Gennep, Turner focuses attention on the tripartite phases of change from one psychosocial state or status to another.[13] In rites of passage from childhood to adulthood in tribal cultures, for example, Van Gennep notes that the first stage involves

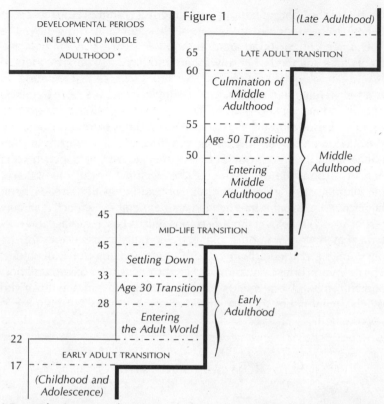

Figure 1

DEVELOPMENTAL PERIODS IN EARLY AND MIDDLE ADULTHOOD *	

(Late Adulthood)

65 — LATE ADULT TRANSITION

60 — Culmination of Middle Adulthood

55 —

Age 50 Transition

50 — Entering Middle Adulthood

Middle Adulthood

45 —

MID-LIFE TRANSITION

45 —

Settling Down

33 —

Age 30 Transition

28 — Entering the Adult World

Early Adulthood

22 —

EARLY ADULT TRANSITION

17 —

(Childhood and Adolescence)

* From *The Season's of a Man's Life*, by Daniel Levinson, et al. (New York: Alfred A. Knopf, 1978), p. 57 Copyright © 1978 by Daniel J. Levinson. Reprinted by permission of Alfred P. Knopf, Inc.

separation of the person being initiated (initiate) from his or her previous ordinary life-world. This is followed by a phase of a separate extraordinary existence that Van Gennep calls *margin,* which is characterized by a stripping of the previous identity and a ritual grinding down of the individual differences of the initiate. After a sufficient period and after the requisite ritual degradations, the sojourn in this state of statuslessness is terminated and the third phase, *aggregation* is entered. This is the time of reintegration and reincorporation of the individual back into the community as a "new" person with a new identity.[14]

Turner refers to these three stages as preliminal, liminal, and postliminal. *Limen* is Latin for threshold, and Turner has adapted from it to designate the limbo-like phase before reintegration as liminal. In a number of important books Turner has sought to clarify the nature and function of liminality in both social and personality process. Like Levinson, Turner emphasizes the natural and normal character of transition states or liminality. Unlike some theorists who lack his overall perspective on the dialectic between society and the individual personality, Turner sees that states of liminality are not only normal, but indeed play creative roles in society, enabling renewal and needed change.

Liminality is one aspect of a dialectical process that characterizes all human societies, a process that oscillates between *structure* and *communitas*. These terms refer to two different social models that Turner believes may be found in any society.[15] Structure refers to society as a differentiated, specialized, hierarchically arranged group of individuals pragmatically organized to aid the group in meeting the challenges of time and history. It includes a status system that makes many distinctions between persons according to rank and social function. Communitas is an expression of society and of social interaction as spontaneous and immediate, relatively undifferentiated, and reflecting a deep, generic human bond between individuals. Liminality, Turner believes, is the occasion (although not the only occasion) for the manifestation of communitas as, for example, in the "unstructured or rudimentarily structured and relatively undifferentiated *comitatus,* community, or even communion of equal individuals who submit together to the general authority of the ritual elders."[16]

When persons are in a liminal state they are "neither here nor there; they are betwixt and between the positions assigned and arrayed by law, custom, convention, ceremonial."[17] Persons undergoing a rite of passage in an initiation or puberty rite, for example, usually have any signs of social status external to the ritual removed and the expected behavior appropriate to the situation is normally passive or humble. "It is as though they are being reduced or ground down to a uniform condition to be fashioned anew and endowed with additional powers to enable them to cope with their new station in life."[18] Part of the purpose of this stripping process is to render the person more open to influence by the sacred, by the creative forces now present that are greater than those encountered in the ordinary, structured, everyday world.

Although liminality and communitas do not express themselves in the same way in modern industrial society as in tribal society, Turner believes that they "break in" to people's modern lives—often in unexpected ways. The recent attention to the very different ideation and behavior common to transition states has helped people to see such states as expressing elements of liminality and often of communitas. We now examine how Turner's concepts may assist in understanding the complex phenomena of alternative religions.

Even though most people have not previously encountered the words liminal or transition state, all of us have experienced some form of the ideation and behavior to which the terms refer. Although Turner has made it clear that modern industrial societies do not package liminality in as recognizable and purely concentrated ways as tribal cultures, modern fragmented liminality expresses itself not only in the "acting out" of adolescents and related seemingly self-destructive behaviors of both adolescents and young adults, but also in the well-known dislocations and often bizarre behaviors of the midlife crisis and in the confusion and passivity that sometimes follows retirement. To say that modern liminality is fragmented is to note that whereas transitioning in a tribal culture might include most of the characteristics of liminality listed in Figure 2, a modern individual's style of thinking and behavior during a transition more than likely expresses only a few. This may be seen as one result of the declining role of public ritual that has characterized the development of modern culture. Related to secularization, this decline of public ritual has not only led to the privatization of religious experience, but it has also tended to set individuals adrift as they enter critical stages of transition in their life cycles or experience the shock of death or other significant loss. Instead of having one's change in situation acknowledged clearly and publicly, with social

50

support and with knowledgeable ritual elders to usher one through the limbo of a transition state, in modern culture one is all too often left to one's own devices, having to seek out social support and "ritual elders" wherever they may be found.

Perhaps the most common but seldom recognized liminal experience is the *grief process*. Since 1944, when Erich Lindemann published his article "Symptomatology and Management of Acute Grief," the topic has received much attention, particularly from mental health professionals and ministers who specialize in pastoral care.[19] Much has been made of the observable effects of the shock of loss—the disorientation, uncritical passivity, suggestability, gullibility, depression, and anger of the grief sufferer. Lack of concern for personal appearance, listlessness with regard to "practical" matters, intensified religiosity, and other apparently strange behaviors look more normal and understandable when seen in the context of the grief process. Granger Westberg has listed the typical stages of the grief process as "(1) shock; (2) emotional release; (3) inability to concentrate on anything but the lost object; (4) symptoms of physical distress; (5) feelings of depression and gloom; (6) sense of guilt; (7) sense of hostility; (8) unwillingness to participate in the usual patterns of conduct; (9) gradual realization that withdrawal from life is unrealistic; and finally (10) readjustment to reality."[20] Westberg goes on to note that although not everyone goes through all these stages or goes through them in the order listed, "many people could have been saved untold hours of agony if they had been told in advance that such grief was normal and necessary in working through to a new plan of living."[21] According to Westberg, there is no way of telling how long a particular person may take to work through this process. Both the individual's constitutional makeup and related typical reactive and adaptive patterns influence the relative speed and relative ease with which a person responds to the life crisis. Westberg has concluded that normally "three months to three years is sufficient time for a person to work through a significant loss."[22]

Westberg's comment about the importance of helping persons to understand that what is happening to them via their "strange thinking and behavior" is really a normal process is true not only

Figure 2
Turner's Categories Related to the Cult Experience*

Psychosocial State Prior to Transition	Transition	Psychosocial State After Transition
— — — — — Movement through normal transitions — — — — —		
Partiality	Totality	Partiality
Heterogeneity	Homogeneity	Heterogeneity
Structure	Communitas	Structure
Inequality	Equality	Inequality
Systems of nomenclature	Anonymity	Systems of nomenclature
Property	Absence of property	Property
Status	Absence of status	Status
Distinctions of clothing	Nakedness or uniform clothing	Distinctions of clothing
Sexuality in marriage and family context	Sexual continence or community	Sexuality in marriage family context
Maximization of sex distinctions	Minimization of sex distinctions	Maximization of sex distinctions
Distinctions of rank	Absence of rank	Distinctions of rank
Just pride of position	Humility	Just pride of position
Care for personal appearance	Disregard for personal appearance	Care for personal appearance
Distinctions of wealth	No distinction of wealth	Distinctions of wealth
Selfishness	Unselfishness	Selfishness
Obedience only to superior rank	Total obedience	Obedience only to superior rank
Secularity	Sacredness	Secularity
Technical knowledge	Sacred Instruction	Technical knowledge
Speech	Silence	Speech
Kinship rights and obligations	Suspension of kinship rights and obligations	Kinship rights and obligations
Intermittent reference to mystical powers	Continuous reference to mystical powers	Intermittent reference to mystical powei.,
Sagacity	Foolishness	Sagacity
Complexity	Simplicity	Complexity
Avoidance of pain and suffering	Acceptance of pain and suffering	Avoidance of pain and suffering
Degrees of autonomy	Heteronomy	Degrees of autonomy

*Adapted from *The Ritual Process* by Victor Turner (Ithaca, NY: Cornell University Press, 1977), p.106. Used with permission.

Examples of Applications in Modern Industrial Societies

Period prior to significant personal loss	Period of mourning—grief process	Reintegration into society after grieving is complete
Settled period of early adulthood	Midlife crisis	Entry into middle adulthood
Period prior to difficulties in early adult transition	Entry into a cult (normal liminality)	Return to ordinary life outside the group
	-or-	-or-
	Remain chronically liminal, unable to reenter structure	Status hierarchy of the group begins to function for the individual as structure

for the grief process, but for other related forms of liminal states as well. Specialists in the psychodynamic understanding of grief have emphasized that the emotional and psychological impact of grief is in fact grounded in the same dynamics as those underlying separation anxiety and other expressions of anxiety related to loss or feared loss of a significant object. All liminal states, then, can be seen to reflect a form of grief process—normal but often bizarre in its forms and traumatic to those experiencing them and to their families. As serious as the death of a loved one is, one should realize that life cycle–related transition states may indeed be even more traumatic. In the transition from one psychosocial state to another the thing that is dying is not just one beloved person, but the entire life-world—the total way of being in the world that has given the person orientation and a sense of meaning for the previous period of his or her life. We believe this rather radical loss provides the necessary context for understanding the complexities of the cult experience and the controversial phenomena related to it.

ELEMENTS OF LIMINALITY IN THE CULT EXPERIENCE

Our thesis is this: For many young persons who enter alternative religions, the conversion—or so-called sudden personality

53

change—either coincides with or follows closely the onset of a life cycle–related period of liminality or transition state. One might say that the sudden personality change *is* the movement over the threshold into liminality. If this can be communicated to the families of such persons, they too may be "saved untold hours of agony" and may be made aware that such transition states are "normal and necessary in working through to a new plan of living." Even the most bizarre reported phenomena of the alternative religions take on a different and much less malignant countenance if viewed as part of a transition process.

Take, for example, the blank, disoriented look that cult members are alleged to have, the trancelike stare that many have suggested results from brainwashing. Where these traits do exist and are not manifestations of drug-related organic brain syndromes, they may be seen as evidence of a continuing state of shock issuing from the trauma of transition. Although grief and related phenomena are *normal*, the severity of the impact of a transition state must not be minimized. After the acute shock has been lessened by the passing of time, the disorientation and confusion may continue for months. This kind of personality change has led many grief sufferers and their families to think that the person is "losing his (or her) mind." This is not usually the case. It is also not the case with most young recruits to religious groups. Some people ask how such a seeming rejection of family desires, values, commitments, and the like could be related to attachment to those desires, values, etc.? The argument usually runs as follows: "If he really liked us, he could not reject us like this—unless someone has damaged his mind. We know he did like us, so someone has in fact damaged his mind." Such a point of view, understandable on a naive level, does not take into account the ambivalence that is present in intense personal relationships. Many times this ambivalence is the source of the anger expressed toward a beloved deceased person. Similarly, it is often behind the hostile, distancing behavior of an adolescent or young adult who is working on personal issues of autonomy and dependency.

Refer again to Figure 2, noting how many of the disturbing characteristics of the participant in an alternative religion find par-

54

allels in the middle phase of a transition process. First, the totalism noted as a trait of many esoteric religious groups is one of the identifying signs of the type of consciousness common to liminal states. Also "normal" to liminal states is a lack of interest in the complexity of issues of critical philosophy and an acceptance of "sacred instruction" that appears, to the outsider, to be simplistic. Gullibility—seemingly uncritical acceptance of and obedience to heteronomous authorities, e.g., the guru—is a recapitulation of the tribal submission to ritual elders and is a contemporary expression of the need for initiating elders/mentors in the maturation process. Ritual submission to a person supposedly possessing extraordinary powers of perception and understanding—usually decried by critics of the alternative religions—has historically been a way that young persons have dealt with the necessity of being initiated into adulthood and is a common characteristic of liminal states. Anti-cultists correctly point out that this submission, dependency, hyperreceptiveness is a dangerous state and one in which it would be easy to take undue advantage of the person who is in transition. We discuss this in more detail below, under the category of *chronic liminality*, in dealing with the possible effects of an unscrupulous guru. For perspective, however, we note here that although such dependency is indeed risky—possibly dangerous—it is not necessarily proof of any psychological malfunctioning, snapping, brainwashing, or the like. A close examination of the actual practice of most contemporary psychotherapies, for example, indicates that psychotherapy itself is essentially a liminal state and that the relationship between therapist and client reveals a kind of submission to the process and dependency on the therapist similar to the guru-chela (disciple) relationship in some alternative religions. Of course, such dependency on a therapist may be foolhardy and dangerous. Our point here is that seemingly uncritical dependency may be seen not as disease process—evidence of brainwashing, snapping, or other malfunctioning—but as a type of relationship common to interpersonal interactions in liminal states that many times are the occasions of transformation and healing.[23]

Various forms of asceticism that appear to be irrational and extreme are also usually characteristic of liminal states. Keeping to a strenuous monastic regimen; working long hours on fund-raising and other seemingly thankless tasks without concern for personal finances; disregard for current standards of personal appearance; eating a minimal, possibly vegetarian diet—all these much-touted evidences of the pathology of group life are in fact normal; standard procedures in liminal states.

Compare, for example, a related strategy for entering a liminal state and being initiated into adulthood: joining the military. A young Marine recruit undergoes ritual humiliations that dwarf anything any religious group can muster. Total obedience and totalism in life-style, hyperreceptivity to the "sacred instruction," acceptance of pain and suffering, long hours, overwork, dangerous activities—many of the common liminal characteristics are present. From our point of view, some join the Marines, some join the Moonies. The reasons and the results are often similar.

Again, notice that in liminal states kinship rights and obligations are suspended. That an individual in such a state seeks to cut off ordinary relationships with his or her family is a natural part of a natural process and need not always be seen as evidence of lack of love, a snapped personality, or a malignant influence. This person may feel that tempting by family members (or their agents) to return to the previous life is "demonic" and may in fact reflect an intuition by the person that such a return might be psychosocial regression. Failed transitions do reflect regression. The only healthy way out of a transition state is the movement to a new adaptation, not a regressive return to a previous state of affairs.

This fact is an extremely important one to ponder before engaging in deprogramming or any other attempt to coerce a person out of a liminal state. Margaret Singer, in her article "Coming Out of the Cults," outlines what she believes to be the problems specific to young persons who have either left a group voluntarily (25% of her sample group) or involuntarily through deprogramming and related activities (75% of her sample). According to Singer,

some residues that some of these cults leave in many ex-members seem special: slippage into dissociated states, severe incapacity to make decisions, and related extreme suggestibility derive . . . from the effects of specific behavior-conditioning practices on some especially susceptible persons.[24]

Noting that "almost all" her informants take from six to eighteen months to "get their lives functioning again," Singer admits that "personal and family issues left unresolved at the time of conversion" remain to be faced, now without the support of the group and its members. Some act out in sexual adventures, whereas others continue their ascetic avoidance of sex. These persons, Singer believes, are characterized by such traits as depression, indecisiveness, slipping into altered states, blurring of mental acuity, and uncritical passivity.[25] From our point of view, this postcult behavior is clear evidence that liminal states are difficult—and dangerous—to terminate forcibly. The behavior Singer reports as characteristic of the ex-cultist and that she blames on the behavior-conditioning practices of the groups is further expression of a continuing state of liminality, one which has *not* been terminated by simply leaving or being coerced into leaving the group. Like grief, this process cannot be terminated at will.

Here again the conclusion is that the traits reported to be present are not only the fault of the religious group, but that the traits reflect psychopathology. We certainly agree that an intensive religious group context is often the *locus* of liminal experiencing, but to conclude that it is necessarily its *cause* is another matter. Such an allegation is an empirical claim and calls for substantive empirical research evidence to support it. Such evidence does not in fact exist. Given the realities of social psychology, particularly the felt need of the ex-member to justify previous behavior with a rationale that exempts him or her from personal responsibility, most researchers agree that testimonies of ex-members as to the causes of their behavior are extremely suspect and should not be presented with the aura of scientific evidence.[26]

We concur that life and regimen in some groups have resources in ritual, meditation practices, time management, etc. for setting and continuing an appropriate ritual context for the "sacred space" and the experiencing of "sacred geography" that is so much a central part of liminal experiencing. Certainly the "stripping" and interpersonal merger, so often part of transition states, do not immediately evidence ego control and ego autonomy in the initiate. As one expression of what has been called "regression in service of the ego," however, it may result *later* in enhanced ego control and ego autonomy. This temporary slipping into less controlled, less differentiated, less rational modes of consciousness has been widely recognized as a prime factor in human creativity.[27]

It must be emphasized here that proving that psychoactive techniques are used by a group is neither proof of malevolent intentions on the part of leaders nor of pathological results. Certainly some ritual techniques are potent for altering states of awareness. Nevertheless, such techniques have been common to rituals of healing that have been ubiquitous throughout the history of human culture and find widely respected use today in hypnosis and other forms. The use of these methods is neither an indictment nor evidence that the average group member will be hurt by them.

Regarding the effects of membership in an alternative religion, there is, contrary to popular assumption, some evidence that participation in one of these religious groups may be beneficial to the participants' psychological and emotional health. Discouraged young people entering alternative religious groups may, for example, feel like social and interpersonal failures, having experienced many disappointments in relationships in their lives before joining. The close, supportive atmosphere common to many groups offers a less threatening environment in which social skills may be tested and practiced. The experience of communitas shared in such a setting de-emphasizes competition and emphasizes acceptance, both factors that encourage new attempts at risk-taking in close relationships. Others find such distasteful activities as fund-raising helpful in overcoming fears of meeting strangers, engaging in conversation with them, and dealing with rejection when it is experienced. The environment in such a supportive group may be likened to what is known as milieu therapy. In the latter a controlled environment, with supportive participants, is used to create a situation in which the patient can experience small successes in living—the small successes without which one cannot move toward confronting the real challenges of the outside world. Scholars have noted the ways in which participation in intensive religious groups and movements has led to effective organizational and leadership behaviors in the secular realm, as participants moved out into worldly pursuits. Rather than ruining their members for a future of success in worldly adaptation, the groups may be helping them prepare to deal effectively with the outside world.[28]

THE PROBLEM OF CHRONIC LIMINALITY

In the discussion above we emphasize that although the majority of members of the new religions are not manifesting mental illness or related conditions of being brainwashed and the like, observers and critics of the groups have indeed noted phenomena that are easily mistaken for pathological symptoms. As we stated earlier, these phenomena are for the most part normal expressions of transition states. We now turn to the issue of the *chronically liminal* members of religious groups. On the basis of our research we have concluded that there are persons involved in the new religions who continue to manifest the ideas and behaviors characteristic of liminal states long after they might realistically have been expected to have finished their transition and moved to the next phase of their lives. That there are such persons in minority religious groups should not be surprising. A long-standing commonplace among specialists in pastoral care is that every congregation—even in the mainstream denominations—has such chronically liminal individuals: those unable to resolve grief reactions; those unable to make the transition into adulthood, into retirement, and so on. The reason for the emphasis on *sustaining ministries* in pastoral care has been precisely that there *are* many such individuals for whom healing may not be a realistic possibility for a number of reasons. Every seminarian who takes the basic course in pastoral care learns the distinctions between healing, sustaining, guiding, and reconciling as expressions of ministry and how to tell when each is appropriate in a given context of ministry.

To gain needed perspective on the phenomenon of the chronically liminal personality in terms of gross numbers of such individuals, there are undoubtedly many times more persons under the care of major denominations than in minority religious groups. Although leaders in the anti-cult movement have suggested that percentages of such individuals are higher in the minority religions, *there is not a sufficient body of quantitative research data to support the allegation.* To substantiate such an allegation one would have to conduct large-scale longitudinal comparative studies involving extensive batteries of psychological tests given to carefully selected samples from large numbers of different congregations and varied minority religious groups. The results would then have to be carefully analyzed, with corrections made for social class, age, and other important variables. From a social science research point of view, such a research project would be fascinating and worthwhile. Given the political implications of such a study in the current climate of paranoia regarding minority religions, it would be extremely important that research on this issue be carried on under the most careful controls against ideological contamination of the results. We emphasize, however, that such careful comparative research has *not* been done, and allegations against minority religions on this issue remain just that: allegations.

THE POWER-HUNGRY GURU

Along with the assumption that members of minority religions are brainwashed zombies comes the image of their leaders as power-hungry gurus. "My child could not possibly have chosen to join this group on her own. . . . She must have been mesmerized, brainwashed, by a hypnotic fanatic guru." As before, we do not question that there are insincere, manipulative, greedy individuals among the ranks of the leaders of minority religions—individuals who have something to gain by keeping members in the group, by fostering dependency and discouraging individual initiative and independent thinking. We do, however, want to challenge the way in which media-hype and those who benefit from it have sought to make it seem that the minority religions have a corner on such unlovely individuals. Anticlerical writers have long performed the service of

60

calling attention to such persons, before and after Elmer Gantry. Pastoral-care specialists have for years called attention to the possible uses and misuses of "transference phenomena" in the relationship between minister and members of the congregation. Even among the most well-meaning group of ministers the temptation toward ego-inflation and related abuses stemming from inadequate understanding of and response to the inevitable personal and group fantasies of a given congregation are an ever-present threat to a responsible professional ministry. The sexual exploitation of parishioners by clergy is a manifestation of the same dynamics and is a recurrent problem in all major denominational groups.

Although such destructive behavior is commonly engaged in by well-intentioned, naive but otherwise normal clergy, leaders who are of a different, destructive genre do exist: pathologically narcissistic characters who feed on their flocks and consider all independent initiative a personal "blasphemous" threat against their rule by "divine right." Clearly, such individuals are dangerous to parishioners and other living things. They should be challenged and, if possible, deposed by their followers or, if the law has been broken, by the proper authorities. Why not more legislation against such leaders? Trying to legislate more specifically against such a phenomenon, as some have proposed, would be an exceedingly difficult and dangerous task. One faction's power-hungry guru is another's dynamic leader. We have more to say about the threat of both antireligious and religious bigotry later. Here it should suffice to note that recent religious bigotry toward and discrimination against Roman Catholics were grounded on the same arguments against nondemocratic leadership styles that are now offered as grounds for legislating against minority religious groups. The complexities of these and related religious liberty issues make it unlikely that dealing with "sick" religious leaders will be made easier by legislation.

The question we must ask as leaders in the American religious establishment is this: How well have we handled the problem of the occasional powerful, successful, pathologically narcissistic pastor, priest, or rabbi in our own organizations? Only after we have given this question careful scrutiny and an honest answer can we see clearly to get the "mote" out of the eyes of the minority religions on this issue. No research exists that indicates such pathological leaders are more common in minority religions than in establishment religious groups, or that indicates establishment religious groups are more effective in winnowing out such individuals from the ranks. Jim Jones was *not* a member of a minority religion; he was an ordained minister in good standing with the mainline Disciples of Christ. Furthermore, secular institutions—including business, government, the military, and the professions—have given little evidence of being able to handle this kind of leader any more effectively than religious institutions. If the American Medical Association and similar professional groups, for example, have such difficulty in protecting clients from incompetent or unscrupulous practitioners, one should hardly be surprised that religious leaders as well sometimes are guilty of abusing power and trust.

Granted that some leaders in religious groups—both minority and establishment—are, given their own pathology, unable or unwilling to assist individuals through transition states back into full autonomy and independent functioning. This phenomenon undoubtedly is a real problem and one deserving of continued concern and attention. However, the powers of such individuals or their ability to hold members in their groups against their wills should not be exaggerated. As seen above, persons undergoing normal transition states may seek out a drill sergeant or a guru to whom they can submit themselves. When a normal liminal state has run its course one of two things usually happens. Either the person turns the Marines or the religion into a career (thereby in Turner's sense reentering structure) or the person leaves the setting of his or her transition state. In the former type of resolution the person remains in the group, usually seeking to achieve status and prestige in the organization through rising through the ranks. Even though the family may not agree with the person's decision, the individual is no longer in a liminal state and can hardly be considered crazy or brainwashed. In the latter type of resolution the individual, no longer needing an authority to submit to, leaves despite the fact that an authoritarian guru may want him or her to stay. In this case the authoritarian guru has no more chance of having his will obeyed than an authoritarian parent.

CHRONIC LIMINALITY AND DEVELOPMENTAL DEFICITS

Why is it, then, that some individuals neither leave the groups to return home nor use the religions institutionally, as a chosen career, seeking to work their way up the status hierarchy of the groups? Clearly, persons in chronically liminal states are of little use even to a hypnotic, authoritarian leader, who has innumerable tasks that must be planned, organized, and implemented if group life is to continue. If a member is disoriented and capable only of minimal functioning, he or she is of little practical use to the group. We have found, in fact, that rather than encouraging disorientation in their members, many times groups turn away from membership those whose emotional state prevents constructive contribution to group life. Certainly, other such individuals continue in group life just as they do in mainline congregations. If the desires of power-hungry gurus have been exaggerated as a cause for these continuing states of debilitating chronic liminality, what is behind this?

Perhaps the hardest thing for anti-cultists to accept is that the severe, extremely debilitating personality deficits they accuse religious groups of causing—where they do exist—are in fact usually grounded in early childhood experiences *within the primary family*. Quite simply, persons who have difficulty negotiating their way through transition states are ordinarily individuals who have not experienced the kind of nurture that leads to the development of a coherent and cohesive sense of self and related strong and effective techniques of ego adaptation.[29] Why were there no problems until the individual left home or college to enter the group? It is a psychological commonplace that severe personality deficits often do not become manifest in clearly recognizable symptoms until the developmental task of leaving the primary family, of *individuation*, is encountered. Then the stresses of separation, object loss—in short, the stresses of major transition—are the occasions on which the developmental weak points in the individual's personality seem to rise to the surface and stand out in bold relief.

63

At this point one can understand that parents would associate the *context* in which the deficits manifest themselves with the *cause* of such difficulties. Faced with the painful reality of a son or daughter who is experiencing severe difficulties in making the transition into adulthood, parents blame variously the schools, the college, a boyfriend or girlfriend, other friends and peers, drugs, television, and in our case under consideration, the religious group that the son or daughter has chosen to join. This is understandable, but our task as religious leaders is to challenge any scapegoating that may be going on. We discuss scapegoating further in chapter 4. Here it should suffice, painful as it may be, to call attention to the fact that severe psychopathology, such as the minority religions are alleged to cause, is almost always grounded in experiences and learnings within the primary family context. Of course, some cases of drug-related brain damage *may* not be directly related to family dysfunction. But here, too, drug abuse and its attendant damage to functioning almost always antedates entry into a minority religion.

In our judgment, persons with deficits in ego function stemming either from early developmental injuries or from drug-related brain damage make up the largest body of those who remain in chronically liminal states within religious groups. If we are correct in this judgment, then we may conclude that these persons create the illusion of the power of the group to hold those in disoriented states against their wills. In chapter 4 we discuss issues relating to pastoral and mental health management of such cases. Here we need only to note that sophisticated mental health teams in reputable private hospitals who have the clear purpose of getting individuals out of the therapeutic milieu and back into normal functioning often have extreme difficulty in returning such individuals to independent functioning. Those who are familiar with the current state of the mental health delivery system are aware that all too often such individuals are doomed to an extremely marginal twilight existence of chronic institutional dependency, often rejected by their frustrated families and lacking anything but minimal public assistance. When such individuals become part of a religious group they remain disoriented, unable to function well, seem to be less themselves than when they remained within the family in earlier, perhaps happier days. Later in this chapter we raise the question as to what realistic alternatives exist currently for such an individual who might be enticed into leaving his or her religious community.

FAMILY SYSTEMS AND THE CULT EXPERIENCE

Because the anti-cult groups style themselves as pro-family and primarily committed to the protection and health of the contemporary family, we find it peculiar that they have made so little of the recent developments in family system theory and family therapy in assessing the significance and dynamics of the cult experience for young people.[30] In all fairness, the tremendous strides that have been made in recent years in understanding family dynamics and the most effective means of assessing and treating dysfunctional families have not been as widely known to the lay public as we might hope. Many mental health professionals remain virtually ignorant about the family systems theory and the new and exciting things it has to teach about "problem children." For the purposes of this book we will only point to some insights that are extremely useful in understanding why some young people may be entering—and remaining in—minority religious groups despite the fact that this choice is extremely painful to their parents and other family members.

First—and for our discussion most important—many prominent family therapists now challenge the idea of viewing the "problem child" as a defective individual who just happens to be a thorn in the side of an otherwise happy family. Rather, the child with behavioral problems is seen as the "identified patient" who has been unconsciously given the role of "problem person" to play in order that the status quo in the family structure not be threatened. In some ways such a child functions as a sacrifice to the family lie—their misbehavior making it possible for the family to function without facing up to some painful truth about its existence. For example, a husband and wife may engage in massive denial of their marital problems, becoming effectively oblivious to their presence. A child has to "act out," keeping them so busy that they do not have time to reflect on their marriage. In effect, the parents *need* the child to misbehave, sometimes even in self-destructive ways. In other cases siblings may have the primary investment in the "problem child" continuing to be a problem. Such a person makes his or her siblings look good indeed, both to parents and community—and this fact is not lost on them. In this light it is fascinating how many times a cult member has a positively angelic, straight, obedient sibling presented by the family as evidence of how "good" and/or "healthy" the family life was.

Undoubtedly, some will cluck that the use of family systems modes of evaluation and analysis in cult-related cases serves only to "guilt-trip" already discouraged families and therefore should not be used. In our opinion, however, family systems analysis should be received as good news for families in such situations, because it offers hope to parents in a number of important ways.

First of all—and perhaps most important—viewed from a family systems perspective, prognosis for a given troubled young adult may be vastly improved. Many disturbing behaviors of adolescents and young adults, examined from an individually oriented point of view (such as psychoanalytic ego psychology), may be assessed as indicating major intrapsychic defects in the personality of the individual in question. Viewed from a family systems perspective, one *need not* conclude anything of the sort. The individual's personality may not be defective at all; he or she may be simply doing a good and creative job of playing an important part in a family psychodrama. How a family views a child contributes to the child's own self-image; therefore, a change in perception of the child based on family systems theory may make a contribution toward freeing the child from his or her alienated situation. This leads to the second reason why family systems analysis should be received as good news in this situation: It radically changes the way in which one views the capacity of other family members to help the alienated family member. If the religious group member is seen as either a brainwashed zombie (a damaged individual) or a psychological defective (again, a damaged individual), usually the family can do little to assist the troubled individual. From the point of view of family systems theory, the best way to help the "identified patient" is to investigate the total structure of the family and to make concrete steps toward eliminating the structural factors within which it makes a dramatic role of "loser" necessary for one of the children. When the family structure changes, amazingly, many individuals considered to have severe psychopathology suddenly stop their crazy behavior (and often a brother or sister begins to screw up . . . but this is another story). In short, the good news is that often there is something the rest of the family can do—and not just sit back feeling helpless.

Finally, the family systems perspective is good news, because it provides a way to understand the relationship between the family life cycle, the problem of individuation, and the phenomenon of otherwise normal young persons choosing to blast away from their family through engaging in behaviors the family considers self-destructive and unacceptable. The period in the family life cycle to be examined closely in this context is what family theorists have dubbed the stage of the family "as launching center."[31] Here the task of the family is to facilitate the individuation of the children from the family matrix, helping them in every possible way to become more autonomous and independent, capable of mature and effective functioning as adults coping with the outside world. Of course, interdependency and constructive relationships with the family are important goals for the person who has completed the individuation process normally.

In the current discussion, however, we take note that in some families the individuation of maturing children is seen as a threat to the existence of the family, and the child is thereby placed in an extremely difficult situation. The child is faced with the choice of remaining docile and submissive to a rigid family party line or of being effectively disowned if too much independence from the will of the parents is shown. Usually the child receives the message: "If you get too independent, we will reject you." Some children respond by continuing to live embedded in the primary family matrix, remaining essentially dominated by the desire for parental approval. These children either continue to live at home or choose to live in a neighborhood close to their parents. Family therapists find that in such cases parents view these children as ideal, normal children

67

and the situation as fine, except for the bothersome surfacing of dependency patterns, which may be experienced as annoying. Parents in such situations verbalize disappointments about the lack of ambition, initiative, independence, and related traits in their adult children—never realizing that the family structure discourages the traits they consciously want the children to have.

There is, of course, another response to such a family matrix that is far more dramatic and disturbing to the family and that we have designated above as blasting away from the family. In this response the child, usually modeling on an aggressive and/or dominant parent, will not stomach continued submissiveness but gradually escalates challenges to family authority structures until the family effectively disowns the child or, alternatively, leaves the child no further options for independent action and self-respect that are not self-destructive or at least drastic measures to prove to the parent that "you will not win." Many examples may be given of such drastic tactics in an individuation struggle. We have already mentioned the option of joining the military against the best judgments of parents. A child can also engage in crazy behavior of various sorts, including drug abuse, self-destructive sexual acting out (sometimes including a stint as a prostitute), getting in trouble with the police in a *creative* variety of ways, and flamboyant failure in parentally approved schools and/or career options.

Against this backdrop of drastic methods of dealing with the task of individuation, joining an alternative religion may seem to some a mild and sensible tactic. Unless the most paranoid fantasies of anti-cultists are accepted uncritically, such a move on the part of a young adult struggling for individuation might seem fairly rational, especially if the offspring is aware of secularist predilections on the part of the parents—or if it is clear that what will *really* get Mom or Dad is their child turning fanatically religious. Being more religious or moral than the parents is an effective way to counter the guilt feelings that usually accompany initiative. A group usually provides not only a place to eat and sleep, but a laboratory to practice personhood in the context of a surrogate family—especially nice if you have flunked out of college and do not have the option to deal with the same issues on campus. Finally, the young person may have decided that putting up with obnoxious gurus, boring meditation, and endless rituals beats drug abuse, jail, or the parents' choice of mental hospitals. If being religious in a weird way ends up bothering the parents more than the other tactics—as is often the case—then this fact just adds icing to the cake.

Certainly this is only one of many kinds of family situations of young persons who have joined alternative religions. However, we have seen this pattern often in our work with families, and it is one example of a situation that can be made intelligible by a family systems perspective without dismissing the problem child as a psychological defective. In many such cases the child's healthy assertiveness is seeking to emerge by way of such drastic measures— not some sinister pathology.

SUMMARY AND CONCLUSIONS

By now one can clearly see that the entire constellation of issues surrounding the question of the psychological dynamics of cult members has been dangerously oversimplified in popular treatments of this topic and in the related media hype. Even many otherwise responsible and well-motivated professionals have uncritically appropriated simplistic anti-cult positions on this topic. Others with more questionable motivations have had much to gain from the continuation and propagation of anti-cult generalizations, and these are discussed in more detail in chapter 4. Here we need only emphasize the following conclusions:

1. There has not been sufficient empirical research study to make any sweeping conclusions about the personalities of young persons who join alternative religions.

2. Because of the variety of organizational, cognitive, and behavioral styles present among the minority religions, studies of one group, e.g., the Unification Church, cannot be assumed to be relevant for understanding personalities in another group.

69

3. Although undoubtedly some persons in minority religions suffer from mental disorders, no existing empirical data demonstrates conclusively either that the group experience *caused* the disorder or that such psychopathology is more prevalent in minority religions than in the same age-group in mainline congregations.

4. Where such severe psychopathology does exist the likelihood is that defects in the individual's ego processes are grounded in early childhood experiences within the family matrix. Certainly such defects may be exacerbated by inept or unprincipled religious leaders, but one can hardly say they have been caused by them.

5. Some behavior of young adults that may appear to reflect defects in psychological structure may reveal nothing of the sort. Rather, the individual may be the symptom-bearer for the primary family, struggling to cope with a pathological family situation and being scapegoated in the process.

6. Some theoretical positions in this discussion are based on the assumptions that secular is better, religious is suspicious, and conversion is snapping of the mind or some other pathological process that should be stamped out at all costs—even, as we shall see, at the cost of religious liberty in America. Professional psychologists of religion have come to no such consensus regarding the nature and dynamics of the conversion experience or of the process of entry into minority religions. Of course, persons with machine models for the functioning of the human psyche are likely to believe much more quickly in the scenarios of mind control, brainwashing, and the like. Similarly, psychologists and psychiatrists of Freudian persuasion tend to share Freud's negative assessment of religion in general and intense religious experience and commitment in particular. Such positions contain a priori metatheoretical assumptions that make negative assessments of much religious experience and behavior before the examination of any concrete data in a given case. In fairness to contemporary psychoanalytic ego psychology, we note that since the work of Erik Erikson there have been many more positive assessments of con-

version and other intense religious experiences among latter-day revisionist Freudians. Thus a *consistently* negative interpretation of conversion experiences is not even regnant within the ranks of scholars and clinicians who are psychoanalytic in theoretical persuasion. One should therefore be suspicious when presented with strident, simplistic characterizations of the impact on young adults of membership in minority religions. If such characterizations are not demonstrated to be based on either the best in contemporary religious scholarship or social scientific research, then one must carefully examine what interests are being served by such gross overgeneralization and consequent irresponsible slandering of thousands of normal—perhaps misguided, but *normal*—young adults.

CHAPTER 3

Deprogramming and the Anti-cult Movement

As a means of responding to the rise of the new religions, the practice called deprogramming claimed (and still claims) the attention of many families who want to get a member out of what they consider a cult. Although not as popular as it was in the mid-1970s deprogramming remains, in the eyes of many anti-cultists, *the* best solution to the cult problem. Despite the many discussions of deprogramming, few attempts to analyze this process have been made.[1] Deprogramming originated with Theodore Roosevelt Patrick Jr., a former community relations consultant to the governor of California. He initiated his efforts after his son had been approached by the Children of God (COG). With other parents of COG members he founded FREECOG (Free Our Children from the Children of God). Within a short time he branched out and began deprogramming members of other groups, including the Church of Armageddon and the New Testament Missionary Fellowship. FREECOG evolved into the Citizens Freedom Foundation, which in turn has given birth to a number of anti-cult groups across the country. These organizations, with such names as Free Minds, Inc., International Foundation for Individual Freedom, and the Personal Freedom Association, form a national network and a contact point between deprogrammers and concerned individuals.

Most people lack information about what occurs in a deprogramming, and much confusion has arisen from the court cases and polemic surrounding the practice. Cult leaders and their supporters have tried to paint it in negative terms—kidnapping, physical abuse and torture, deprivation of freedom. Deprogrammers have tried to picture it as merely an opportunity for extended dialogue. Recently, many deprogrammers have been reluctant to discuss what happens in a deprogramming, for as the Rev. Joel MacCollam correctly reflects, "the cults have used such information in the past to program their people against deprogramming."[2]

Despite the difficulty of putting together a picture of a typical deprogramming, several substantive accounts of some deprogrammings have appeared. If used with some awareness of the biases of the authors and the distortions that have entered into the accounts because of the deprogramming event itself, these accounts (Christopher Edwards,[3] Kent Levitt,[4] Bernie Weber,[5] Barbara Underwood,[6] Arthur Roselle and Wendy Helander[7]) offer a coherent explanation of the process as it developed in the late 1970s.

From its informal days of the early 1970s deprogramming has become a profession. Family members who wish to have a person deprogrammed contact a deprogrammer through an anti-cult group. The typical person interested in a deprogramming is a parent of an adult son or daughter. (Parents retain direct control over minors and most new religions will not accept them as converts without signed parental consent.) Parents hire a deprogrammer as their personal agent.

Deprogrammers are self-appointed professionals. There is no educational process through which a deprogrammer must go nor any set of professional qualifications he or she must meet. The deprogrammer need only declare himself or herself in business and begin to receive clients. Although a few deprogrammers we have encountered do have psychological or other graduate academic training, the majority are ex-cult members (or their immediate family) who have been recruited during a deprogramming session in which they participated.

The first step in the process—getting the cult member to the deprogramming—involves some form of forceful detention. Some families have used conservatorship laws (originally drawn up to protect the affairs of elderly people who are senile), but most courts no longer award custody of an adult to a family for deprogramming. Thus families and deprogrammers are left with what amounts to kidnapping. In some cases they accost the person on the street or as he or she is leaving a place of employment. More often than not, they interrupt a family visit at home during a holiday or weekend visit.

Deprogramming has two distinct goals, although the distinction becomes blurred in the process. First, deprogrammers hope to wean the individual cult member from the group and destroy any allegiance to the group that might remain. This goal is uppermost in the early stages of the deprogramming. After winning over the cult member, deprogrammers hope to return him or her to what could be called a normal life (in the eyes of the persons paying for the deprogramming). The second goal is more difficult to attain.

After the kidnapping—which is peaceful to the extent that the individual does not resist the captors—the deprogrammers rush the person to an isolated, physically secure place, often a motel or an isolated private residence previously prepared. All the windows are locked and nailed shut as a standard security measure. Ted Patrick, early in his career, noted that "they all tried to go out the windows at the first opportunity."[8]

Once in place, the deprogramming proper begins. Deprogrammers emphasize the centrality of rational dialogue in the process. In fact, the major event in the deprogramming consists of lengthy conversations in which the deprogrammers try to tear apart the belief system of the person being deprogrammed. Barbara Underwood, a former member of the Unification Church (now married to deprogrammer Gary Scharff and a deprogrammer herself), said deprogramming consisted of a calm dialogue between her and her deprogrammers, former Moonies whom she respected. What is deprogramming according to Ted Patrick? "Essentially it's just talk. I talk to the victim for as long as I have to. I don't deny that that's the catch for many people—for as long as I have to!"[9]

74

Such a picture of deprogramming, as essentially talk, is consistent with the view of the process that anti-cultists articulate. They believe that the cults capture the *minds*. Cults more or less subtly *program* members much as a computer is programmed. Thus, individual members are under some form of mind control and can no longer think for themselves or make rational decisions. Two popular anti-cult authors speak of members having their mind "snapped" and as a result are suffering from an information disease, involving impaired awareness, irrationality, disorientation, and delusion.[10] Ted Patrick, who has done more deprogramming than anyone else, believes that cults hypnotize people. "I tell the parents, 'You're not dealing with your son at this point. You're dealing with a zombie. *You have to do whatever's necessary to get him back.*'"[11] Recently he told a *Playboy* interviewer:

> PATRICK: After a year in a cult, the members' minds cease to be, and they develop a mental condition, and they become a vegetable, or suicidal. . . .[12]

MacCollam views deprogramming as an effort to restore the cult member's ability to make personal choices, apart from the influence of the group or its members.

In truth, deprogramming appears far more complicated than Patrick, MacCollam, or other deprogrammers would have people believe. It is far from simply talk. It involves a complex, pressured massage of the person's total inner life. Ministers and skeptics alike have for ages known the fruitlessness of trying merely to argue a true believer out of a position. More is required. At least seven well-defined pressures recur in the accounts of the deprogramming process.

1. Environment control. Deprogramming begins with the physical confinement of the cult member. Not only is this confinement sudden and unprepared for, but it carries with it the threat that it will last until the deprogrammers have accomplished their goals. Patrick reflected that although the average deprogramming takes less than a week he told a stubborn Bernie Weber, "I've got nothing else to do. I can stay here three, four months. Even longer. Nobody's

75

going anywhere."[13] Thus the deprogrammers place the cult member in a completely controlled environment and future.

2. *Privacy.* Besides being cut off from familiar and friendly surroundings, the cult member loses his or her privacy. Someone stays with him or her (often sleeping in the same bed) 24 hours a day. Kent Levitt, admittedly strongly hostile and resistive to his captors, was blindfolded and chaperoned whenever he went to the bathroom.[14]

3. *Sleep.* Time for sleeping is strictly limited during deprogramming. Patrick sees lack of sleep as an essential element to his work. Levitt relates long sessions in which he would doze off only to be screamed at, shook awake, or made to get up and walk.[15]

4. *Personal abuse.* Throughout the deprogramming the person is psychologically attacked and is told she or he has been misled, foolish, and a failure. In many cases, when resistance is strong, verbal abuse is stronger. As Patrick recalled during the *Playboy* interview, he told one girl:

> PATRICK: Girl, you're a bitch. . . . You're sitting there looking more like a man than your two brothers. You're in a cult that took a beautiful girl and made a lesbian out of her. . . . You take orders from that no-good son of a bitch, you will eat his shit. . . .[16]

Arthur Roselle has described one of the most noteworthy cases involving alleged personal abuse. While finishing a visit to his parents' home he was seized by several men and thrown to the tile floor. He was tied and placed on a cot. He remained tied for three days. According to his affidavit, his deprogrammers worked on him in shifts and even threatened to subject him to a series of shots if he did not begin to cooperate.

Two conditions particularly irked Roselle. First, he said, was that he remained tied whenever he went to the bathroom, which was a pot a neighbor helped him urinate into. He was too embarrassed to defecate. During the days he was tied, a number of people came into the room where he was confined. He noted, "Some talked to me, some just came and looked at me. I was unclean and unshaven, my clothes were messed up, and I was either tied to a chair or to the cot." Now a militant anti-deprogrammer, he remembers those days: "The experience was designed to humiliate me."[17]

At this point of attack on the person being deprogrammed, lack of formal training or understanding in psychological processes can be dangerous. If the deprogrammer works from the naive assumption of "freeing the victim's mind" instead of the more realistic notion of psychological manipulation, he can do great damage. Having accepted an ethic that says anything is legitimate to deprogram a cult member, the deprogrammer can exacerbate any existing emotional problems.

The untrained deprogrammer, bound by no code of professional behavior, can become dangerous if the cult member's resistance to the deprogramming leads to frustration, anger, and anxiety about the possible failure of the deprogramming attempt. Those cases of physical abuse of deprogrammed victims that have surfaced seem to be directly related to the victims' hostile reception to confinement and resistance to the deprogramming. Attempts to escape, for instance, many times bring retaliation and confinement with ropes. In isolated cases severer abuse has been reported. Such cases may be infrequent, but once a deprogrammer accepts the idea that the end result of deprogramming makes any means allowable, then he or she opens wide the door to abuse.

5. *The invasion of sacred space.* As part of their attempt to destroy the group's standing in the eyes of the believer, deprogrammers denounce and ridicule the individual's participation in what the group considers holy. This attack often helps objectify the group in the member's mind. (It can also strengthen the person's identification with the group, especially if the group assigns high status to "suffering for the faith.") Because many groups assign a special cosmic, even deific, role to their leaders, deprogrammers will tear up pictures of gurus. In the sessions with Bernie Weber a picture of Sun Myung Moon was defaced into a caricature of the devil.

Walter Taylor, an Old Catholic monk, reported that his monastic garb was ripped off, his crucifix taken away, he was not allowed to perform any of his daily worship routine, his prayer life was held up to ridicule, and he was encouraged to eat foods forbidden by his faith.[18] The eating of forbidden food has been a significant part of the deprogramming of members of the Hare Krishna, because they have the most strict diet regulations of the new religions.

6. *Parental pressure.* The attack on the emotions during deprogramming is most evident in the participation of parents and family members. Not only are they involved for the legal protection of the deprogrammers, but as Patrick notes, they are also helpful psychologically. "The victim has a constant pressure on him from parents, reacts subconsciously to their constant expressions of love, their unhappiness over his condition, their tears."[19] Barbara Underwood's mother, an almost constant companion of her daughter during her deprogramming, shared how God had pulled her through the years of separation and rejection by Barbara during her years in the Unification Church and encouraged Barbara to take up activities not part of her church life.[20] Christopher Edwards' father was a constant and active part of his son's deprogramming. After dinner one evening Chris's father said to him, "You know how much your mother and I love you. She's behind this a hundred percent. I've been in touch with her by phone every few hours. She misses you terribly." Chris noted his reaction: "I tried to picture my mother's face. I tried to remember my old life after seven months of trying to block it out. All my old loves and hates . . . my home, my family."[21]

7. *Interrogation.* Rational dialogue is part of the deprogramming, but more often than not the dialogue takes the form of an intense interrogation, with several people taking turns engaging the cult member in a session of diatribe, badgering, leading questions, and theological and biblical dialectics. Few persons of any faith would be able to counter all the arguments that could be brought against the practices of their faith, and few cultists are informed enough to understand the rationale for all their group's rituals and

beliefs. Isolated and surrounded by deprogrammers, the individual faces intellectual attacks on her or his belief system, ridicule of unusual patterns of behavior, and the continual presentation of symbols of the benefits of the life that was left to join the group.

The net result of all the practices of the deprogrammer is to wear down the cult member's resistance to accepting the deprogrammer's views. The practices cause physical and emotional fatigue and create a strong sense of humiliation and guilt. The controlled environment produces a sense of hopelessness. Cut off from the group, the confined individual is alone. Eventually, the wearing down prepares the imprisoned member for the presentation of a way out: "conversion" to the deprogrammers' world view and acceptance of the deprogrammers' goal. Frequently, in a successful deprogramming, this conversion is as instantaneous as a sinner being saved at a revival meeting. In the *Playboy* interview Patrick describes it:

> PATRICK: Then there'll be a minute, a second when the mind snaps back and he comes out of it. The only way I can describe it is that it's like turning on the light in a dark room or bringing a person back from the dead. It's a beautiful thing, the whole personality changes, it's like seeing a person change from a werewolf into a man. . . .[22]

The breaking point for Bernie Weber came after an emotion-filled session during which his father reviewed months of correspondence between Bernie and the family. Seeing his father weeping and being accused by him of trying to kill his grandfather and of inflicting great anguish and pain on the family, Bernie was forced to answer the question, "Who do you love more? That pimp (i.e., Moon)—or your father?" Caught up in the emotion of the moment, Bernie embraced his father and gave the answer they were all gathered to hear.[23]

The breaking, the ending of the formal deprogramming, does not end the session; it merely accomplishes the first of the goals: breaking the allegiance of the member to the group. After the deprogramming the professionals advise a further rehabilitation period. During this time an ex-cult member is said to *float,* that is, he or she remembers life in the group, longs for its security and benefits, and considers returning to it. Some anti-cultists consider floating a dangerous emotional state of uprootedness and instability. In any case, this floating time is crucial, for if the ex-member is left unattended, he or she may bolt and return to cult life. Ideally, an ex-member spends weeks or months in a rehabilitation center with other ex-members who function as a support group. During this time the deprogrammers encourage the ex-member to tell his or her story to others and even actively recruit the individual to assist in other deprogramming attempts.

The time it takes for the new "conversion" to become integrated into the personality as a continuing reality (i.e., the length of the floating period) varies tremendously. Patrick noted in the *Playboy* interview:

> PATRICK: Some float for two or three days, others float for two or three months. Some never recover. . . .[24]

AFTER THE DEPROGRAMMING

The period immediately after a completed deprogramming is usually filled with tension. Everyone is aware of the floating phenomenon. Often the group attempts to contact the deprogrammed member. Many leaders in the new religions know that even the slightest contact can provide the support an individual might need to withstand the pressure of the ordeal. They also feel a certain responsibility to assist, if possible, in rescuing the individual from the deprogrammers, whom they regard as negatively as the deprogrammers view them. Such attempts at contact usually bring cries of harassment from parents and family, especially if they receive repeated phone calls or have members of the group watching their house.

Social scientists recognize deprogramming as fitting into their understanding of the psychology of hostages. In fact, deprogrammers seem to have rediscovered, almost as if by accident, the technique of "breaking" prisoners in such a way that not only is the will to resist demolished, but the prisoners actually come to love and support their captors' aims. Compare the case of Patty Hearst. Spirited from her house one evening, she was subjected to all the pressures of a hostile environment. Locked in a closet for weeks, raped, subjected to a barrage of rhetoric on the Marxist beliefs of her captors, she cooperated eventually and was reborn as Tanya, a fully committed member of the Symbionese Liberation Army who had over the weeks "freed her mind" from the "programming" implanted by her wealthy environment.

As noted earlier, deprogramming has two goals: to get the person out of the group and to return her or him to what the parents or whoever finances the deprogramming consider a normal life. Although the majority of persons who go through deprogramming are weaned away from their groups (we have no figures on which to make a definite statement), by no means are all deprogrammings successful in the second instance. In this section we look at the variety of outcomes of deprogramming attempts.

Wendy Helander and Steve Post are members of the Unification Church. Peter Willis is a member of the Episcopal Church. Debbie Dudgeon is a Roman Catholic. Arthur Shiva Dayan is a member of the Sivananda Yoga Society. What they have in common is that each has gone through an attempt physically to coerce him or her out of his or her faith and each has returned to the group as a witness to the fact that deprogramming does not always work. Wendy Helander, whose story has received national media attention, was abducted three times by her parents and on each occasion (once after 85 days) returned to the Unification Church.

Steve Post was awakened from his bed in his parents' home and taken to an isolated farm on Long Island. He escaped after six days of deprogramming. He returned to the Church, attended and graduated from the Unification Seminary, and is currently a doctoral candidate at the University of Chicago Divinity School. Debbie Dudgeon, Peter Willis, and Arthur Shiva Dayan could relate similar tales.

Within the Unification Church, Hare Krishna, the Way, and other groups that have been major targets of deprogramming attempts, such persons take on special roles. They are the contemporary equivalent of first-century Christian martyrs. They have suffered for their faith. Because of the parents' actions they have also experienced lengthy, if not permanent, breaks with their families.

As mentioned above, the return of persons who have been through the trauma of a deprogramming to "normal" lives is more difficult to attain than simply eliminating their involvement in or allegiance to groups. That so many do not (or cannot) return to normal existence is strange if one accepts the deprogrammers' understanding of what they are doing. Seemingly, if they are returning the capacity to think, to make decisions, and to accept parental love, the individuals should be able to return soon to normal existence.

Some persons do return to normal lives. They marry, settle down, and develop careers. However, most frequently these seem to be those already on the fringes of the movement. Rachel Martin seems to be such a person.[25] She was swept up into the nomadic Jim Roberts' group. During the months she spent with this group she developed doubts about the gap between what actually happened in the group and the image the group had of itself. Within a few hours of her being captured she had made her decision. As she described it, "God deprogrammed me." The few arguments used by her deprogrammers seemed irrelevant; they merely confirmed her own thinking. She has since married, returned to school, and is seeking a career in nursing. A similar story seems to be the case of Alison Cardais,[26] who was "deprogrammed" by her father on the plane returning to their suburban Chicago home.

The stories of Rachel Martin and Alison Cardais seem to be exceptions. Ellen Lloyd, Gary Scharff, and Barbara Underwood are part of a large group of persons who have been deprogrammed. On "breaking," after expressing conversion to the truth being given to them by the deprogramming, they were immediately recruited and joined the deprogramming movement. Subsequently, they have become professional deprogrammers. The work within the movement has taken the place of a dedicated life within their former groups and manifests all the characteristics of religious devotion. Their former lives are denounced as evil, and their deprogramming is held up as a lifesaving event and their present work as a godly crusade. They have, in other words, exchanged one totalistic commitment for another.

Cynthia Slaughter's life is illustrative of this type of experience. She joined the Unification Church in 1975. After only six weeks as a member she encountered Ted Patrick. After her deprogramming she and her father formed the International Foundation for Individual Freedom, headquartered in Arlington, Texas, and she quickly became a leading voice in the deprogramming movement. In 1976 she was among the speakers to address the first of the cult hearings conducted by Sen. Robert J. Dole (R-Kans.). She spent the next few years on the lecture trail and working in a rehabilitation center for people who were floating.

Then, quietly, in 1978, she packed her belongings and returned to Denver, where she had first joined the Unification Church. She was a Moonie again.

In Ted Patrick's interview with *Playboy* he characterized another group who have gone through deprogramming: "Some never recover completely." Patrick refers to the deprogrammed individuals who cannot readapt to "normal" lives. For some, deprogramming results in a disorientation toward life that leads to long-term psychiatric care or even institutionalization. Sometimes it has led to suicide.

Recently one of us was interviewed by a television station that was presenting a series on cults. Among others interviewed was a recently deprogrammed Moonie. The day after the series was shown the young man left the rehabilitation center and returned to the Unification Church. The next day his mother went to the Unification Center and got him out again. Caught in the middle, the man wound up in a mental institution. Although not true in the majority of cases, long-term psychiatric disorders that follow deprogrammings occur too frequently to be written off as singular, odd coincidences. In the following chapter we provide a framework for understanding the relationship of this phenomenon to the psychology of transition states. Here it should suffice to note that deprogramming is clearly *not* just talk leading to a confrontation and freeing of the mind; it is a direct traumatic attack on the entire system of psychological and emotional defenses of the individual. Any existing emotional problems can be exacerbated as the psyche of the individual becomes a battleground between the group and the deprogrammers.

Viewed in its narrow ideological framework of "freeing people from mind-control situations," deprogramming approaches cultists naively, neither understanding the complex set of concerns that lead people to join alternative religions nor noting the benefits that the groups may have offered in meeting these concerns. If these concerns are not addressed, the needs that led to the joining of the group in the first place remain and will probably lead to subsequent problematic involvements. For some, these needs are met by joining the deprogrammers, who offer a sense of mission and purpose and a program to act on. Others drift into other cults. Some vegetate and a few commit suicide.

Deprogramming thus presents a mixed picture. Sometimes it works and produces the results families and deprogrammers desire. On many occasions, however, it fails. Where it has failed completely it has usually produced serious long-term disruption of family ties and has become a monumental barrier to bringing families split by religious differences together again. In other cases the process has precipitated or intensified existing psychological problems and has led to long-term hospitalization or even suicide. We conclude, therefore, that the psychological harming of someone through deprogramming seems a major reason to seek after alternatives.[27]

Early in the 1980s deprogramming began undergoing a revision under the impact of controversy and criticism. Many deprogrammers have been embarrassed by incidents of violence, such as the reported rape that occurred during a recent attempt to deprogram a young woman from Cincinnati. The term deprogramming has come to be used for every kind of face-to-face anti-cult activity. This more general connotation of the term in recent usage reflects partly a genuine attempt by some to move the cult member into a counseling situation and partly a public relations attempt by some anti-cultists to mask the violent element of deprogramming they perpetuate.

In either case, deprogramming remains a questionable activity. At best it involves forceful detention and the imposition of the deprogrammers' opinions and values on the person being deprogrammed. To pretend that a person being forcibly detained is prepared for a rational discussion with a group of deprogrammers is pure fancy. Thus even with recent attempts to modify the process, we can find no justification for it and in the next chapter suggest alternatives designed to protect both the person who chooses to follow the path of a different religion and the high value we place on family life and intrafamily relationships.

FROM DEPROGRAMMING TO AN ANTI-CULT MOVEMENT

Deprogramming, involving as it does the forceful abduction of and coercive action against its victims, created widespread controversy. By the mid-1970s proponents and opponents began to align themselves on either side of the issue, and what had started as a minor attempt by a few parents to get their offspring out of cults became a national movement.[28]

A national coalition emerged in 1973-74, as Ted Patrick began to run into trouble. A number of people whom he had attempted, unsuccessfully, to deprogram took him to court on kidnapping and civil charges. No major convictions or fines were levied, but legal fees mounted. Patrick expanded his efforts beyond the original Children of God in southern California and now reached clients across the country.

In 1975, having depleted his financial resources in the cause of deprogramming, Patrick decided to leave his job with the state and began making a living as a deprogrammer.

This same year the original group of parents of Children of God members (FREECOG) gave way to the Citizens Freedom Foundation headed by William Rambur and James Crampton, two parents whose daughters Patrick had attempted to deprogram, without success. Citizens Freedom Foundation was the first of several groups to spring up around the country and create what would become, in 1976, a national network of deprogramming organizations. As Patrick was joined by other "professional" deprogrammers, these organizations served as the promotional arm of their business, and they actively solicited clients needed to keep Patrick and others in business. With the emergence of deprogramming as a commercial venture, economic concerns began to dictate policy. The spread of deprogramming efforts to locations around the country increased expenses markedly as did the legal fees resulting from the rising number of people bitter about being kidnapped and subjected to a week of deprogramming. The process became more elaborate and added the lengthy rehabilitation period, which caused expenses to escalate further. As costs increased, the number of parents of cult members who could and/or would pay thousands of dollars to a deprogrammer and risk subsequent legal action decreased. New clientele had to be found.

The movement then fed on strong existing tensions within social groups, to provide a base on which a new clientele could be developed. In 1978 Flo Conway and Jim Siegelman called on deprogrammers to target all born-again Christians. Some deprogrammers had already expressed opinions about deprogramming all Mormons, Jews, and other classic minority groups. Other deprogrammers had discovered that deprogramming could be used against anyone for almost anything. By the time Conway and Siegelman were writing, deprogrammers had already moved against an Episcopalian, several Catholics, Baptists, two Greek Orthodox, numerous Evangelical Christian groups, and a Hasidic Jew. Not confining their efforts to cults—or even religion—deprogrammers turned to members of ideological political groups. Attempts were made to deprogram a young wife whose mother disapproved of her choice of a husband, and, more recently, a young woman accused of lesbianism.

Deprogramming has become a tactic that can be used against any person who follows any activity not approved by his or her family. Deprogrammers, in effect, can define their clientele as *anyone willing to pay the fee.* Operating with a much lower profile as the 1980s begin, deprogrammers and those who support them morally and financially have institutionalized and attempted to legitimize a tactic of social control that has no place in a democratic society.

LEGAL ISSUES AND THE ANTI-CULT MOVEMENT

As mentioned in passing, the controversy over deprogramming led those involved to the courts. It has gone far beyond, to major legal and legislative battles that are being waged even now. The cult war found its most heated expression on the legal front, as court battles gave way to attempts to pass anti-cult legislation. Court battles were initiated as both individuals and religious groups reacted to what they considered illegal and/or discriminatory action against them.

As might be imagined, members of alternative religions, viewing themselves as adults with wills of their own and the right to exercise these wills, resented deprogrammers abducting them, locking them up, and putting them through the ordeal of deprogramming. Several of Patrick's early failures turned on him with a vengeance. The first, Dan Voll, a member of the New Testament Missionary Fellowship, charged Patrick with unlawful restraint and kidnapping. Patrick appealed to the legal principle of justification, which allows one to break the law in some instances to prevent an immediate and greater harm, and was acquitted. However, the next year Patrick was convicted twice, once on charges of false imprisonment in Colorado and more recently for kidnapping in California. As a rule courts have been reluctant to convict on kidnap or other felony charges.

Frustrated with criminal cases, the victims of deprogramming shifted their emphasis to the civil courts. Two factors contributed to this shift. First, deprogramming groups discovered in many state laws the provision for what is termed a conservatorship, in which the state appoints someone to see to the affairs of an individual deemed incompetent to manage her or his affairs, with the understanding that if a safeguard were not established, the individual might be duped out of her or his assets. Originally, conservatorships were intended primarily for older people moving into senility, but temporary conservatorships had been granted in cases where, for example, blood transfusions were deemed necessary to save the life of a child of a Jehovah's Witness (a denomination that does not approve of blood transfusions).

Members of deprogramming groups began assisting parents to obtain conservatorship court orders as a means of getting legal custody for a deprogramming effort. Once the court order was obtained—almost always without an appearance by or even the knowledge of the person against whom the conservatorship was granted—the deprogrammers were free to take custody of and deprogram an individual without fear of legal reprisal.

Second, victims of deprogramming attempts turned to the civil courts as an alternative. They attacked the practice of deprogramming as a violation of civil rights in general and denounced the use of conservatorships in particular. Because of their efforts, most states quickly stopped the practice of appointing conservators. The major victory in the civil courts came in 1977, as a result of a class action undertaken by the Way International against the Freedom of Thought Foundation in Tucson, a center to which many persons were taken for deprogramming and/or rehabilitation. The center was closed and its managers ordered to cease and desist from deprogramming activity.

In the fall of 1978 the first civil rights case between deprogrammers and their victim was settled. The court awarded $10,000 to Dan Morgel against both his deprogrammers and his parents. Subsequently, a number of civil cases have been filed. Some have resulted in definitive decisions, such as the Wendy Helander case. Wendy became the focus of the national media after her three kidnappings and attempted deprogrammings. She filed suit in civil court, charging violations of civil rights and denial of First Amendment freedoms. In return, her parents sued the Unification Church, claiming that it engaged in hypnoticlike recruitment techniques that rendered new members unable to choose between competing alternatives. In the former case Wendy was awarded a sizable settlement and the deprogrammers ordered to cease bothering her and engaging in deprogramming activity. In the latter case the court found no evidence to support the contention of the Helanders and dismissed the suit.

Interestingly, the major effect of the court cases, despite the numerous decisions against the deprogrammers, has not been on the legal front; many deprogrammers, as vividly illustrated by Ted

Patrick, have simply ignored court orders. The litigation has hampered the deprogramming effort by markedly increasing costs, because a significant amount of money has to be paid out in legal fees, and deprogrammers are often involved in legal proceedings.

The frustration of the various deprogramming and anti-cult groups in the courts—which increasingly ruled against them and almost never supported them beyond tossing suits against them out of court—led them, in 1976, to seek legislation that would either curb the cults or provide legal sanctions for deprogramming activity. They found an early ally in Sen. Robert Dole and with his assistance put together an informal legislative hearing called "A Day of Affirmation and Protest." In this public forum the anti-cultists presented their case against the new religions. Senator Dole declined to invite any representatives of the groups attacked to appear or later present their responses in writing. Although a transcript of these hearings was printed and widely circulated, no legislative action resulted.

Two years later, however, the groups returned to Senator Dole, who agreed to hold further hearings in Washington, DC. Wide publicity made these hearings a matter of intense controversy. Like the original hearings, no provision was made for any speakers to present responses to the anti-cultists' attack. Nevertheless, because of the pressure from some mainline religious denominations and civil rights groups, such as the American Civil Liberties Union and the Alliance for the Preservation of Religious Liberty, at the last minute Senator Dole consented to give equal time.

The Dole hearings were given added life and notoriety by the events in Guyana, which occurred just weeks before the hearing. Both Guyana and the Dole hearings spurred efforts by anti-cult groups to promote legislation at the state level. Efforts to move against selected alternative religions began in Rhode Island, Connecticut, Pennsylvania, New York, Ohio, Illinois, and Texas. In most cases a bill was introduced and legislative hearings held. These hearings produced heated debate but no positive legislative response. The major exception has been New York, where the Lasher Bill—which would have sanctioned conservatorships for deprogramming—passed the state assembly on two occasions and was blocked from becoming law only by the governor's veto.

To date, despite numerous attempts, anti-cult groups have failed to get a single piece of legislation passed. To a large extent their failure must be attributed to the opposition given such legislation by civil rights groups, black and other minority groups, and the national leadership of some mainline churches, all of whom have seen the wider, dangerous implications of such selective legislation.

The legislative and court phases of the controversy have come together on the local level, where many of the alternative religions have engaged in public solicitation and fund-raising. Most notably, Hare Krishna groups became quite active in selling books and flowers at airports, and the members of the Unification Church spread out in mobile fund-raising teams to sell flowers, butterflies, and other trinkets. Both groups were accused of deceitful selling techniques, and the Krishnas became objects of intense animosity for bothering travelers at airports.

Responding to citizen protest, city councils across the United States, acting mostly out of ignorance of court rulings about solicitation, passed antisolicitation measures directed against the Unification Church and the Hare Krishnas. The enforcement of these new ordinances led to literally thousands of court suits, and in almost every case the court ruled in favor of the religious groups. In a few cases the court also fined members of city councils for conspiracy to discriminate.

These legal moves against the alternative religions run counter to attempts to maintain religious tolerance and pluralism as well as the rights of religious groups to function in the United States without encountering discrimination. Given the record of court rulings this century and the record of anti-cult groups in the past few years, it seems unlikely that any substantive support for anti-cult legislation will emerge. Still, as has been learned from history, the stirrings of religious discrimination are never to be taken lightly or underestimated. As seen below, at least some responsible leadership on these matters has been forthcoming.

THE RESPONSE OF THE CHURCHES

When controversial issues arise one expects the church to offer its counsel. In this case it has spoken clearly and with a surprisingly united front. On February 28, 1974, the Governing Board of the National Council of Churches issued a statement opposing deprogramming and declared it a violation of religious liberty. (See the complete text in Appendix B.) In strong language, the resolution stated that the forcible abduction and protracted efforts to change a person's religious commitments violated not only the spirit of the United States *Constitution,* but also the Universal Declaration of Human Rights, which guarantees the right to change religious beliefs and to manifest this belief in public activity.

Since this time other church bodies have followed the National Council of Churches' lead in opposing deprogramming and attempts at legislative activity by deprogramming groups. Representatives of seven church bodies—the United Methodist Church, the United Church of Christ, the United Presbyterian Church, U.S.A., the Unitarian Universalist Church, the Church of the Brethren, the Lutheran Council U.S.A. (which speaks for several Lutheran bodies), and the Baptist Joint Committee on Public Affairs (which speaks for a number of Baptist bodies)—along with the Synagogue Council of America, protested the Dole hearings and the government's attempt to regulate or suppress minority religions, i.e., the so-called cults.

Likewise, on a state level, many prominent church leaders have come forward in opposition to anti-cult legislation and have spoken forcefully against attempts to curb unpopular religion. Those most opposed to anti-cult legislation have noted that its defeat usually follows quickly on the churches' becoming vocally involved in the issue. For example, Roman Catholics, once the target of Protestant groups who saw them as a threat to public peace and safety, have arisen to condemn the attackers of the minority groups. In Pennsylvania, where legislative hearings on anti-cult bills were held, the Pennsylvania Catholic Conference condemned such action as a threat to religious liberty. In the Jesuit periodical *America,* Fr. Richard A. Walsh cautioned readers to "be slow to accept the statements of hostile parents and disillusioned former members of the church. We should be alert to the propaganda being disseminated by the enemies of all religions."

As various attempts to legislate against the new religions at the state level emerged into the public eye, ecumenical agencies joined denominational leaders in protesting the state's interference in religious life. In this endeavor they have followed the lead of the National Council of Churches and the church bodies that protested the Dole hearings.

Ecumenical and denominational leaders have been joined by theologians and religious scholars (both of whom have been noticeably absent from the deprogramming groups). At a meeting convened by the Anti-Defamation League of B'nai B'rith, spokespersons for the 22 scholars concluded that the new religions pose no threat to society but need to be examined because of their ability to meet people's needs in ways the mainline churches cannot provide.

The church has been caught on the horns of a dilemma as the deprogramming controversy has heated up. Within Christian circles there is a history of opposition and polemics against heretical and non-Christian bodies. This polemic, this defense of Christian teaching and ministry in contrast to alternatives, is an altogether fitting and proper task when carried on within the boundaries of civil liberties and Christian ethics. But the question remains, how does one offer a critique of one's religious neighbors without crossing the line of denying or infringing on their right to exist, worship as they see fit, and propagate their faith?

We personally have lived with and agonized over this dilemma. Defending the right of alternative faiths to exist has, in the heat of the anti-cult polemics, been too easily seen as agreeing with their specific faiths and practices and condoning their mistakes. In some cases this blurring of distinctions has been done by those involved in the anti-cult movement as an attempt to discredit their opposition. These are two distinct questions. Criticism of alternative religions must continue, but such criticism and dialogue must be accompanied by action taken to preserve their legitimate rights in American society.

CHAPTER 4

Responding to the New Religious Pluralism: An Agenda for Action

If one is not to take the stance of the militant anti-cult movement and support deprogramming and other concerted action against minority religious groups, then what are the alternatives for responsible leaders in both church and community? On the basis of the above discussion, one can see that a phenomenon as complex as that of the new religious pluralism requires an equally complex and nuanced response. In this chapter we present an overview of the various arenas in which religious pluralism and its impact have to be addressed as well as some concrete suggestions we believe might be helpful in each arena, from the wider community to the family context. We address issues of public education in the realm of religion and family life, responsibilities of the church at both denominational and local levels, and finally, practical considerations regarding the management of family conflict around religious issues.

Even though the so-called cults are not nearly as numerically large as some media treatments have led people to believe, religious pluralism is becoming an increasingly important reality in society. This would be true even in the best of times. In times of social and economic stress the importance of this phenomenon becomes more evident and not simply because of the possibly greater attraction of religion in bad times. In his *Escape from Evil* Ernest Becker has argued convincingly that we human beings are constantly searching for ways to bolster our fragile self-esteem, to reassure ourselves of the potential success of our wildest dreams, to protect our fantasies of wholeness, success, and immortality from recognition of the realities of brokenness, failure, and death.[1]

Becker's powerful psychocultural analysis has widespread significance for theologians and for specialists in the human sciences. His understanding of the human propensity to project the guilt and blame for one's own failure is especially important in view of the contemporary cultural and religious situation. Becker believes the denial of one's own shortcomings and eventual death is directly tied to the demonic tendency of human beings to search for "sacrificial victims" whose very existence explains why things (families, the economy, personal and/or professional projects) do not work out as hoped. The continual human quest for scapegoats—all too often on a genocidal scale—is directly grounded, Becker is convinced, in people's personal and collective unwillingness to face up to their failures, their guilt, and their starkly limited sojourn in this world. Erich Neumann, in his *Depth Psychology and a New Ethic*, has argued a similar point.[2] We as human beings, he maintains, will be unable to advance in social ethics until we confront effectively our penchant for projecting our own unacceptable qualities onto an available target person or group whom we then seek to isolate or, if possible, to destroy and thereby "deal" with our own problems. Indeed, we are familiar with this phenomenon and recognize it as one of the primary factors that led such an apparently civilized nation as Germany to turn its advanced technology to "a final solution." The Holocaust, of course, is the paradigmatic example of the phenomenon of scapegoating. Nevertheless, if one had hoped that the shock of the death camps would turn people away from using this tactic, then one should note the trends toward questioning—not just the human propensity to monstrous evil, but the very historical reality of the death camps. One can see why Becker questioned whether human beings will ever give up such

94

"useful" tactics for demonic self-deception. In short, the old bigotry was never defeated, despite recent fantasies to the contrary. The increasing number of anti-Semitic incidents in this country and in Europe, the continuing sectarian violence in Northern Ireland, and the recent regression in race relations in the United States are clear cases in point.

THE NEW BIGOTRY

The rise of the militant anti-cult movement in America marks a new chapter in the history of human bigotry. *The new bigotry turns both the ideology and the new scientific perspectives of the Enlightenment into the effective tools of ancient scapegoating.* The use of modern science and technology to aid in the scapegoating solution was pioneered with great energy and effectiveness by the Nazis. Similarly, Amnesty International has documented extensively the manner in which the Soviet government has utilized extensive anti-cult legislation and "legal action" against political and religious minorities in the Soviet Union. That Russian mental health professionals are employed as part of the enforcement arm against dissidents is a widely accepted fact. Nevertheless, most people have never really believed that Nazi Germany and contemporary Russia have taken Enlightenment-based, liberal democratic principles as fundamental to their existence, and people have not really been surprised at their misuse of medical and social scientific knowledge and power. The emergence of the new bigotry in American culture is a particularly troubling development for this country's democratic society, because many of the people who traditionally sounded the first alarm at signs of social scapegoating now remain, at best, relatively silent. At worst, they have become active supporters not only of dangerous anti-cult (and ultimately, antireligion) legislation, but also of the political use of establishment psychiatry and the mental health delivery system. In short, the current and as yet unchecked tendency to medicalize the phenomenon of minority religions rather than face changing cultural trends constitutes a clear and present danger to democratic processes and related religious

95

liberties in American culture. Church leaders—both liberal and conservative—have recently had their capacities for rational, logical, civilized discourse taxed to the utmost by arguments over the supposed significance of the "new religious right" and related issues, such as abortion. The ad hominem arguments, hysterical exaggerations, and scurrilous attempts at character assassination that often accompany discussions on abortion, for example, do not provide much basis for hoping that discourse on the appropriate responses to the current religious pluralism will fare any better. Indeed, there are indications that serious, rational public discourse on religious pluralism and related issues will be even more difficult. On the abortion issue, for instance, large groups with articulate and influential spokespersons exist on both sides, ensuring at least a semblance of due process. On issues surrounding minority religions, however, those who might be expected to defend due process for social minorities have in one way or another absented themselves from this concern. The establishment denominations, while taking an occasional but little publicized denominational stand, have been preoccupied with other issues deemed more pressing, have provided little leadership at the national level, and have often supported the anti-cult movement on the local level. America's Jewish community, long the most vigilant segment of the population concerning infringement of religious or personal liberties, has not readily come to the defense of other minority religions. There are, no doubt, many reasons for this, paralleling the various preoccupations of the churches. Combine legitimate concern over the future of Israel, the situation of Soviet Jewry, and the larger proportion of Jewish young people recruited into some of the minority religions and one has at least some perspective on the relative lack of Jewish leadership in protecting the religious liberties of other minority religious movements at this time. Concern within the Jewish community about evangelical Christian groups who had targeted Jews for conversion in the early 1970s led directly to concern about Jewish conversion to cults. Led by the Department of Interreligious Affairs of the Union of Hebrew Congregations, some Jewish leaders became deeply involved in anti-cult activity and actively promoted the Lasher Bill. They found support for their activities by tying the cult issue to traditional Jewish opposition to practices of proselytizing and conversion, even though the religious groups that have made the largest inroads into the Jewish community have been those which are the *least* evangelical in recruiting new members.

Jewish support of anti-cult activity has been countered within the Jewish community by significant support for the rights of alternative religions to exist and function. Jewish leaders like Rabbi Daniel Polish, who signed a statement against the Dole hearings, and Constitutional lawyer Jeremiah Gutman have been leading spokespersons against anti-cult activity that violates the civil rights of alternative groups and their members. Various Jewish groups, taking the long-standing position of the Jewish community in support of minority rights, spoke out unequivocally against the Lasher Bill in New York. Obviously, the war against the cults has made for strange bedfellows among its leadership, encompassing both Jewish leaders who oppose the cults' proselytizing among Jews as well as certain evangelical Christian leaders who are themselves interested in converting Jews. At this point, it suffices to note that conflict within the Jewish community has at least limited its traditional effectiveness in defending minority rights.

The American Civil Liberties Union (ACLU) remains one of the few traditional defenders of due process that clearly struggles to ensure that minority religions do not currently end up as the most available sacrificial victims. Jeremiah Gutman, head of the New York branch of the ACLU, expressed disbelief at the lack of assistance by established religions in the ACLU's struggle to defend the rights of minority religions. From his point of view, even if the established religious groups can muster no moral outrage in this struggle, their very self-interest is so great that their lack of interest and support is shocking.[3]

Finally, the traditional, more humanistically oriented liberal community—usually on the forefront in such a struggle—has been almost neutralized on this issue. The secular humanists, often misinformed about religious phenomena and usually uninformed by the best in contemporary religious scholarship, become easy prey for those who would reduce religious conversion to a pathological phenomenon easily domesticated and "handled" by a mental health professional. Such individuals find it difficult to see either the implicit ideological basis for their "diagnosis" of minority religionists or the pseudoreligious quality of their own secular humanism.[4] Here again, American anti-intellectualism, particularly regarding religious issues, has contributed to the emergence of the new bigotry. Ignorance has always been a prerequisite for effective scapegoating. In projecting one's own undesirable characteristics on the other person or group, it is convenient if there is a bit of truth in the accusations—even more helpful if there exists in the person or group a substantial "hook" for one's projection.[5] But if an individual's demonic intention is to use the other as a receptacle for unconscious projection, to depreciate the other in a totalistic way, to rob the object of any complexity or humanity that might otherwise inhibit aggression toward one's own most disowned characteristics, then ignorance of the object which is to receive the projection clearly becomes the most essential ingredient in the psychocultural brew that issues in scapegoating.[6] An ancient insight, manifest in many religious traditions, maintains that the devoutly religious person is among those most susceptible to the temptation of spiritual pride. Accordingly, projecting one's own spiritual shortcomings often becomes the special demon of intensive religious communities and of the religious virtuoso. Indeed, religious wars and polemics of the old bigotry have this particular dynamic as one of the primary engines that drive them. In fact, this remains the primary psychology behind the vicious, sadistic attacks by contemporary, premodern religionists on the devotees of other religions as well as the devotees of various denominations of secular humanism. We continue to see expressions of this phenomenon, not just among militant fundamentalist Muslims, but among some (and we emphasize *some*) more orthodox or conservative Christians and Jews, particularly in certain branches of the anti-cult movement and the pro-life crusade against abortion.

The phenomenon we are calling the *new bigotry* is not a temptation to more orthodox or conservative religionists; indeed, one might say it is culturally unavailable to them as a potential response.[7] Rather, those who consider themselves children of the Enlightenment—militant secular humanists, arrogant reductionists, and in-

98

tellectually and ethically proud liberal religionists—are the most susceptible to the temptations of the new bigotry. Because their goal is often to be "more secular than thou," they shrink from the epithets of "pious," "religious," etc., as if to be tainted with religious experience or conviction is to be tarred with the most abhorred brush of all. As contemporary Jungian interpreters of modern secular culture would put it, *the shadow side of modernity—that which is most feared and disowned—is consciously realized and affirmed religious experience that issues in a serious commitment to a symbolic life.* In the new bigotry, individuals exaggerate, depreciate, and otherwise caricature the religious life of others to avoid confronting the spiritual dimensions of their own lives in a conscious manner. Also, ignorance or superficial knowledge of the history and phenomenology of religions serves as fertile soil for the caricaturing of a religious life the observer experiences as irrational or alien. In the old bigotry the traditions and practices of others are studied not to understand but to find the vulnerable spots where an attack might be most effective. In the new bigotry we find that the vast literature of religious scholarship is usually conveniently ignored.

Global generalizations about religious individuals or groups—including minority religions—become increasingly difficult in direct proportion to the degree of familiarity with the scholarly literature on a given individual, tradition, or religious practice.[8]

Behavioral scientists in general and psychological interpreters of religion in particular are among the worst transgressors in their quest for relatively simple explanations for vastly complex phenomena. Although this may be initially surprising, a close look at the training required for doctorates in the behavioral sciences, either theoretical or applied, reveals the educational reasons for simplistic psychological treatments of cultural and religious phenomena by such individuals. One can become a psychiatrist or a Ph.D. psychologist with little or no training in the humanities in general and with no grasp of the technical philosophical literature necessary even to understand the hermeneutical problems involved in a psychological interpretation of religion, much less to offer adequate generalizations regarding religious personalities or communities.[9] Although generally true of university professors in these fields, it is

99

even more evident with the typical counselor or psychotherapist. One should keep this in mind when faced with pronouncements by mental health professionals on the meaning and "real significance" of religious experiences and behavior. This is not to say, of course, that there are not individuals in these various fields who have done their homework in philosophy and religious studies. These are the exceptions, however.

Clearly, we in the church find it difficult to become intelligent consumers of psychiatry and psychology in relation to issues that affect us, partly because we project our fantasies of competence, even omnicompetence, onto professionals in these areas of specialization. Psychology has become the religious authority for many secularized modern individuals both in and out of the churches. Mood-control drugs have taken on the role of the Eucharist, and psychotherapy has become the most popular form of practical spirituality for those who can afford it.[10] We must, however, become more responsible critics of our fantasies in order to make appropriate use of mental health professionals and not expect sophistication in areas in which most have not been trained. When, for example, members of these professional groups offer pronouncements regarding cultural and religious phenomena that have widespread public implications, their credentials to speak in these matters must be carefully evaluated, as well as the adequacy of the research (if any) that lies behind their interpretations. Also, we must voice the question our liberation theologians have taught us to ask—that of the *interest* underlying the interpretation.[11] As seen above, such careful examination usually leads us, not to simple explanations or global generalizations, but to an awareness of the complexities involved in any attempts to offer an interpretation of a religious movement, belief, or practice. Let us turn now to highlight a resource that we, both in and out of the church, have failed to utilize as effectively as we might in the context of the current situation.

PUBLIC EDUCATION AND THE NEW RELIGIOUS PLURALISM: THE IMPORTANCE OF RELIGIOUS STUDIES PROGRAMS

The last few decades have witnessed a quiet revolution in the study of and teaching about religion in U.S. colleges and universities. In earlier times the study of religion at the college level reflected the cultural hegemony of Judeo-Christian traditions and usually involved studies in the Bible, church history, and Christian theology at church-related colleges. State universities for the most part did not organize departments of religious studies, partly because of hesitation based on a narrow reading of the church-state issue. Today religious studies programs across the nation have multiplied and been significantly strengthened, not only in private colleges but in many outstanding state universities as well.[12] In fact, departments in state university settings now produce some of the best-known and most highly acclaimed scholarship in the study of religion. In our view this increasing attention to the public study of religious traditions is appropriate and timely. Fortunately, the increasing number of academic programs in religious studies accompanies a broadening of the curriculum to reflect the reality of global religious pluralism and to address the methodological complexities inherent in understanding the phenomena of human religious experience. In contrast to the previous situation, religious studies are no longer limited to investigations of the Judeo-Christian tradition. Instead of ignoring other major religions of the world or lumping them together in a one-course survey of world religions, the stronger departments now give equally careful attention to other major traditions of the world. Recent emphasis on the history and phenomenology of religions in graduate programs has produced a new generation of scholars who are sensitive interpreters of Hinduism, Buddhism, Taoism, and other faiths, not just of Christianity or Judaism.[13] Major religious practices, such as conversion, meditation, sacrifice, prayer, and pilgrimage, are studied in a comparative way and from a perspective that includes insights from many different historical periods, cultural contexts, and religious traditions.

New attention to the social scientific study of religion supplements this historical breadth of approach. Work on the contributions of cultural anthropology, sociology, and psychology to the study of religion is carried forth and evaluated as to the limitations of these approaches in understanding the human religious experience. For example, much attention is given to the understanding of conversion in world religions from an interdisciplinary point of view.

A number of things should be noted regarding the significance of these programs. First of all, it will be important in the coming decades that the educational level of the American public improve in relation to religion and religious issues as they influence society. The new religious pluralism has brought with it not only more religious options for young people, but also a greater likelihood of conflicts centering around religious differences and related value issues. People *will* be confronted by religions other than their own. The question is, How will they respond to these situations? The contribution of religious scholars will provide a key resource in future years. Access to the best available information will be of the utmost importance in avoiding either uncritical acceptance of a given group's self-promotion or uninformed—even bigoted—stereotyping and caricaturing of the faith of other people.

Some have sought to introduce a broader approach to the study of religion in the public schools, but they have met with only limited success. Clearly, the main source of credible information continues to come from the colleges and universities. Students should therefore be encouraged to take courses in religious studies in order to develop the capacity to evaluate their various religious options.

As an expanding diversity of religious commitments manifests itself in various public ways, these religious scholars play a more important role as consultants to legislative bodies, mental health professionals, churches, and other groups.[14] The use of religious scholars is already noticeable but must be encouraged by leaders in various public sectors if their contribution is to be optimal. Although some legislators, as well as some groups of mental health professionals, for example, already consult with religious scholars in areas where they lack expertise, too many continue to make important decisions based on popular misconceptions fostered by the anti-cult movement and dispersed by the media.[15]

Some departments of religion still lack members with any expertise in religions outside the Judeo-Christian tradition, but the American Academy of Religion has moved to encourage curriculum change that takes into account the current religious situation. Many colleges and universities, however, have not yet seen fit to develop a program in religious studies. Given the current cultural and religious situation, such an omission is an irresponsible, perhaps dangerous one. Civic and religious leaders should encourage the appropriate educational leaders to include such programs in college and university curricula and to give the necessary support to leadership in this area. In sum, the need for reliable information on diverse religious traditions and practices will increase, and therefore, the academic resources that can generate such information must be developed and supported.

THE PUBLIC CHURCH AND THE NEW RELIGIOUS PLURALISM: CHALLENGE AND RESPONSE

Before leaving the topic of the importance of education for dealing with these issues, we want to raise the question of how theological educators should respond. If the public church is to respond effectively, its pastoral leadership will have to be prepared. Strangely, the seminaries lag behind the colleges and universities in this matter. In fact, seminaries tend to discourage students from taking extensive work in religious studies before enrolling in seminary. In a simpler cultural era, when the curriculum of college religion departments paralleled that of seminaries, most theological educators believed that a seminarian could learn all that was necessary while in seminary and that a solid liberal education would, therefore, be sufficient preparation. Certainly, a broad undergraduate background in the sciences and humanities continues to be desirable for a seminary-bound student. If a student, however, chooses a career as a religious leader and does not study the varieties of religious traditions and experiences before enrolling in seminary, how will such a scholarly foundation be developed? Clearly, individuals in situations of religious conflict often turn first to the minister—sometimes the only resident religious scholar in a given town or community—for both information and counsel. The pastor, therefore, must either provide or facilitate congregational educational programs relating to the contemporary religious situation. Without a strong undergraduate concentration in religious studies,

103

including solid work in the history and phenomenology of religion, preparation for this challenge is left to the seminaries.

Few seminaries, however, offer study in the history and phenomenology of religions outside the Judeo-Christian tradition. Of the courses that are offered, many caricature other faiths from a narrow confessional stance that seeks not to understand and value, but to debunk and dismiss. Usually, seminaries have no faculty member with credentials to teach the history of religons. A crowded three-year curriculum has no room for offerings that seem extraneous to preparing ministers for the Christian church and its ministry. We are arguing, however, that becoming a responsible religious leader in this culture at this time requires a basic literacy in the history and phenomenology of religions. A pastor, of course, cannot usually become a specialist in Hinduism or Buddhism or in the various other traditions that make for the new pluralism. But he or she should have a working knowledge of both major and minority traditions and should know where to find more specialized information if it becomes relevant in a given pastoral situation.

Probably the best place to get such a foundation is in a good religious studies program at the undergraduate level. Barring such preseminary preparation, ministers should seek remedial work in the area during seminary and continuing education afterward.[16] To counter the old or the new religious bigotry with reliable information, the pastor needs to be prepared to provide local leadership. We will return to other tasks of the pastor in the local congregation and community, but at this point we need to address the task of the public church in providing leadership on this issue.

Given the recent political and economic developments in the United States, the various denominational hierarchies are more burdened than ever. Still, we emphasize that the major denominations provide practically no leadership on this matter at the national level. Although some denominations have issued important public statements on religious liberty in the context of the alternative religions, they have made little effort to educate denominational constituencies regarding the issues involved. Clergy in a number of mainline denominations remain unaware of their churches' positions and consequently become uncritical allies of the anti-cult movement.

104

For example, we have repeatedly encountered pastors who have had no communication from their denominational leaders on this topic and who have therefore turned to the only known "experts" on the topic—pop media or journalistic treatments or representatives of a "the-cults-are-coming," pro-deprogramming perspective.

Most denominations have national offices responsible for interfaith dialogues; clearly, they should assume the burden of leadership. To neglect other faiths in question would be to continue the same denial of cultural realities typical of the past. Significantly, it is a cadre of some of the most creative systematic theologians and other religious scholars, and not the denominational leaders, who are confronting the issues involved in depreciating other faiths and their adherents-issues that have so many pastoral ramifications. But it is not in the halls of academe that this interreligious conflict is most critical, and the academicians alone, no matter how active and dedicated, cannot offer the leadership required to prevent the most destructive effects of a potential new wave of religious bigotry and related conflict. Denominational leaders must provide local churches with resources through educational curricula that offer guidance in these situations.

First of all, we in the mainline Protestant churches need to admit that we are doing a poor job of assisting our congregations in general and young people in particular with their practical spirituality.[17] Only recently have most Protestant seminaries begun to wrestle seriously with spiritual formation for seminarians, i.e., assisting them to find meaningful ways of assessing their own lives and the lives of others through religious reflection, as well as to explore the nature of spiritual nurture through prayer, meditation, and other forms of spiritual discipline and direction. We have tended to identify such pursuits as pietistic, "mere human religious strivings," privatistic, individualistic in a negative way, and leading to a lack of involvement in the worldly tasks of the church. This perspective reveals the shadow side of the professional model of ministry. Urban Holmes, Kenneth Leech, and other leaders in pastoral and spiritual theology have noted that reducing the ministry to a profession carries with it grave implications—primarily in its not so subtle implicit secularization of ministry. The movement away from

105

the vision of ministry as first and foremost *religious* leadership has led to the much discussed identity diffusion of the clergy and has left lay people without pastors who are comfortable in the role of spiritual guide for their congregations.[18]

The increasing tendency to bifurcate the individual and community, the private and public dimensions of the church's ministry, and the consequent association of concern for spiritual direction and practical spirituality with the merely individual and private is not only misleading, but destructive of ministry to both individuals and society. Unless persons are assisted in what Charles Winquist has called *practical hermeneutics*—that is, in interpreting the meaning of their lives before the Sacred, in the context of an *unconditional horizon*—they may never experience a transformation of perception that could enable them to see what the divine initiative would have them do in response to the needs of their global neighbors.[19] The phenomenon of burnout is a reality not only for clergy, but also for laity who have been discouraged from seeking contact with the living waters through prayer and other traditional spiritual disciplines. Adolescents and young adults, especially, need sensitive help in developing what Matthew Fox has called a worldly "creation-centered" spirituality.[20] If we in mainline Protestant churches do not help our young people by modeling a serious commitment to a life-affirming religious vision and praxis, then we should not be surprised that others step into the vacuum we in our smugness have created.

Second, we need to reevaluate our tendency to depreciate any attempt to offer young people options for religious life and ministry that are costly—*sacrificial*—for them and that give them an opportunity to explore the "meaning of meaning it."[21] One of the things that has especially angered parents is the willingness of their young people to offer themselves freely to lives which do not focus on building a successful upper-middle-class professional career. Even time spent in the Peace Corps and in Vista—secular counterparts to high-commitment ministries—has often been viewed as "wasted" by ambitious parents.

Clearly, we need to challenge the tendency of parents to view their children merely as self-objects, extensions of themselves through which wounded self-esteem and failed aspirations may be made good. This is a widespread dynamic and one which—although understandable—cannot be condoned or allowed to go unchallenged by Christian proclamation. The splitting of the children into the "good one who may fulfill my dreams" and the "bad one who is the cause of my frustration and disappointment" is a common destructive pattern in families. Such a dynamic can easily lead to family conflict in the area of the worth of religious commitment, particularly if a child is experimenting with "the meaning of meaning it." Not only should we educate about and bring judgment to bear on this destructive family pattern, but we must also seek ways to offer young people our own high-intensity, high-commitment *sacrificial* opportunities for religious living, communal or otherwise.

Third, and obviously related to the above, we in mainline churches must highlight the nature and stages of the *family life cycle* in educational programs. For families who have or will soon have a late adolescent, we need to emphasize the task of preparing the child for individuation from the primary family. We have tended to celebrate the idea of the family's staying together rather than acknowledge that a young adult must necessarily differentiate himself or herself emotionally from the previous position of psychological merger with the family. Certainly, positive relationships and constructive communication and interaction between the family of origin and the young adult should continue. But we have a moral responsibility to assist families in the process of giving psychological birth to their maturing children. There has been little education on this developmental perspective on families, and our church education leaders must begin to provide it.

Fourth, while realizing that some young adults will not have been adequately prepared for "birthing" from their families of origin, we must ask what we as churches are doing to provide "developmental sanctuaries" often needed by such young adults if continued healthy development is to be facilitated? Many young adults have attained a developmental stage at which they no longer can tolerate the controlling aspects of the primary family matrix, and yet they lack sufficient resources to function independently as adults. This situation is more common now, as economic problems cause increasing employment difficulties for young persons. Many, for example, have sought independent status outside the family home but then find themselves faced with the seeming necessity of moving back into the house with disappointed parents. This problem has been with people for a long time, but it is an especially important focus of contemporary ministry to young adults. Many of the minority religions have offered young persons in such situations a supportive environment complete with food, housing, and in effect, a laboratory to practice social and adaptive skills. This is, of course, the traditional idea of a halfway house, which has long been viewed as an important resource for those who need support and encouragement as they attempt to get on their feet.

We need to face frankly the abysmal situation that exists nationwide regarding the availability and quality of such way stations on the journey toward adaptation. The mental health delivery system has never been adequate in this area, but the situation has deteriorated into a little-publicized or little-recognized crisis situation, with the recent trend toward "dumping" mental patients out of large hospital settings. Health-care entrepreneurs have moved into the breach, and here, as in the related nursing home industry, the abuses are common and scandalous. For a young person who has had psychiatric problems—whether involvement with a minority religion has been part of the case or not—locating a decent, let alone therapeutic, halfway house environment is extremely difficult and often impossible. The difficulty increases in direct proportion to the person's or family's inability to pay the enormous costs usually charged by centers that adequately qualify as therapeutic, growth-facilitating environments. This problem is addressed later, in discussing issues to be faced when attempting to find such a facility for a young person leaving a group or considering leaving it. At this point, however, we would simply emphasize that major denominations have tended to concentrate their health-care and social service involvements in other areas and have given little attention to needs of this kind.

In response to this situation, the church could design its own developmental sanctuaries to meet the needs of young persons at various points on the developmental continuum, offering them

108

meaningful involvements in ministry and/or community living appropriate to their psychosocial situations. Seminarians would make excellent residential staff for such centers, and such involvements would provide opportunities for important clinical experience while offering an important social ministry. The American Association of Pastoral Counselors could provide the various denominations with technical consultation on such ministries, assistance with staffing, and ready contact with other professionals needed to develop such programs.[22] The possibilities for providing creative ministries to and through young persons who are having trouble leaving home are exciting, but they will never become realities without the catalytic function of denominational leadership. The resources needed to create and experiment with such way stations for young persons are considerable and therefore beyond the reach of most single congregations. Models must be designed, tested, and publicized, so local communities will not be faced with the task of meeting these needs without access to the learnings of those who have gone before them. Presently, *some* of the needs are being met by alternative religions. *Can we as mainline Christians afford not to put denominational funds and other resources on the line in facing up to these needs of young people?*

Fifth, some theologians and other religious scholars see the Christian encounter with other religions as crucial. The church at the local level, however, has tended to lend its assistance to a paranoid, xenophobic response to the minority religions. This response and related attempts to suppress the alternative groups have had the effect of strengthening the very groups they seek to destroy (Christians, of all people, should understand this). Taken together, the persecution the groups have experienced and the hysterical media treatment have given the groups more strength and influence than would have resulted from a more balanced and informed and less bigoted response.

As Christians, we must raise the question of our operant theory of change, of how we may best influence the behavior of others in a democratic society. Certainly we have theological and ethical criticisms of most, if not all, of these minority groups. Some groups, undoubtedly, do have corrupt leaders who manipulate and exploit group members. Some groups have questionable sexual ethics, particularly notable in their depreciation of women. Some groups do engage in unethical business and financial practices. No doubt some engage in practices that may jeopardize the health of their members. Of course, these and other negative characteristics of religious groups are not limited to minority groups. When they do manifest themselves in an alternative religion, or when there seem to be sound reasons for concern and investigation into a questionable activity or practice, then we must first gather accurate information to avoid being party to unfounded accusations and the sort of rumor-mongering that so often characterize allegations against minority religions. Also, we must keep in mind the fact that because one group may have engaged in, for example, deceptive recruiting practices, this does not mean this sort of irresponsible behavior is characteristic of all groups. We have the responsibility of bringing criticism to bear on all cultural forms, including our own. If we are serious about wanting to influence the groups to change their behavior or practices in areas that offend our ethical commitments but that are not against the law, we have several options. First, we can seek to enact legislation to force the majority's behavior and ideological values on religious minorities through police power. We have discussed recent attempts to do just this. The temptation to pursue this response to the minority religions and others who differ from us on religioethical issues will be a continuing one, we believe, despite recent setbacks.[23] This is a dangerous response, primarily because of the implications for the ultimate erosion of religious liberties.

Second, we can seek to isolate the groups through religious ostracism. This is the approach of those who refuse to take part in any dialogue with representatives of a minority religious group because such contact would "lend credibility" to the group. Many take this view—some out of the not-so-subtle classism of the old "church-sect" distinction, some because they would not want their reputations besmirched by association with "marginal people" who have negative status quotients, and still others because a leader or leaders of a particular group have been the target of allegations of criminal or unethical behavior. Advocates of this point of view, we believe, should reflect on this approach in the context of Christian

110

theology and ministry. Such a response cannot be justified within the frame of a Christian perspective on ethics and ministry. We must consider the wider implications of modeling such a response to "troublesome presences" within our society as an acceptable— even preferred—response to such individuals. Recently, in both Europe and the United States, such approaches were used to support established racial and religious bigotry. Surely we have learned enough not to sanction this response to the alternative religions.

The other option available to us if we desire to influence these groups is open communication with them. A dialogical model carries with it the risks inherent in the democratic process. One may be changed through such interactions—perhaps even be convinced by others that their wisdom or faith is superior to one's own. Without such dialogues there will be little opportunity to understand the alien, and without understanding, little opportunity to influence the practices that trouble us. Here confrontations can be made, challenges offered, ethical issues discussed in a public forum. This is neither a pipe dream nor an idealistic fantasy. This process has already been initiated by many courageous mental health professionals, social scientists, religious scholars, and clergy from establishment denominations across the country. It is a model that has had significant results not only in increased understanding, but in facilitating reconciliation within families and in challenging those patterns and practices on both sides which heighten paranoia and hysteria and which feed destructive interactions.[24]

Besides direct dialogues with minority religions through their representatives, public discussion of related issues must be facilitated at all levels of church life. For example, the centrality of changed immigration laws in creating the current religious situation has been noted. One must realize that the issues of alternative religions in American society cannot be separated from public policy issues centering on immigration. Indications are that a debate on immigration is emerging which will be socially devisive. Medicalizing the problem as the anti-cult movement has done will not make the new situation go away. We in the church must prepare ourselves for countering a new wave of nativism and xenophobism that may be severer than in 19th-century America. Again, rational discussion on these issues will be extremely difficult and will strain our leadership resources. Still, we in the public church must not shrink from our responsibilities.

COPING:
GUIDELINES FOR HELPERS AND FAMILIES

Representatives of the helping professions often see families as they experience turmoil centering around issues that present themselves as religious conflict. Too many helpers have been the victims of the misinformation promulgated by the anti-cult movement and have been recruited as uncritical supporters of activities against minority religions. These include pastors who have not evaluated the wider implications of their actions for religious groups in general; pastoral counselors who, of all therapists, should be prepared to counter simplistic treatments of religious conversion as pathological but are not; psychiatrists and psychologists who have had insufficient academic background in philosophy and religious studies to understand either the complexity of the issues involved in making generalizations about religious phenomena or the verbalizations of clients who may be members of minority religions; and finally, therapists whose orientation focuses on intrapsychic processes without giving sufficient emphasis to the importance of the context of the personality—the family system. These and related issues have been addressed above, along with the educational task that includes informing mental health professionals of the complexities of understanding the cult experience. The urgency of this educational task is obvious. Before concluding this book, we want to offer some practical guidelines and answers to common questions that may be useful to both professionals and relatives of persons who have joined alternative religions.

One of the most tragic effects of media sensationalism and anti-cult hysteria is the way in which parents have been led to believe the worst about alternative religious groups, about the prognosis for their children, and about their inability to do anything short of hiring deprogrammers. The situation is more complex and far less destructive and hopeless than many think. We offer the following guidelines for parents who agree with us that deprogramming is an unacceptable option.

1. *Remember that you are not helpless in this situation, that there are things you can do.* Although it is tempting to believe the worst, your child is probably not a zombie, the victim of brainwashing, snapping, or the like. Such dehumanizing stereotypes of group members are questionable and appear to have little or no validity. Clearly, such a decision by a young adult is a significant one, and one that should (indeed, probably is *designed* to) get your attention. It is not a time to become hysterical, but a time to focus your thoughts and energies.

2. *Present no ultimatums and engage in no attempts to intimidate your child into reconsidering.* Parents tend to indulge themselves in tantrums at this critical point, forgetting that their power to influence behavior this way is limited, if not nonexistent. Usually, parents in such situations have not welcomed independent thinking or behavior on the part of their offspring and have browbeaten adolescent and young adult children into submission or silence. *The most important asset you can have in the coming months or perhaps years is your ability to keep the lines of communication open.* If you have already severed communication or feel your child has forced an end to communication, read on.

3. *Find out what group has been joined, and then research it.* Seek out accurate information from scholarly sources you can depend on and that have not been designed to scare you. Obtain information about the group's origins and its belief system, major assumptions, practices, and so on. Such information is usually available through sources noted in this book. Language spoken by your child that seems crazy and unintelligible may be easier to "translate" and understand than you think.

4. *Communicate Interest and willingness to discuss.* Keep your conversations honest but not hostile. You need not agree with or approve of the group's beliefs or your child's involvement in the

113

religious group. What *is* needed is a communication of respect for your son's or daughter's right to engage in such an endeavor. Many young people are already discouraged to the point of despair. This new religious involvement may be one of the last desperate moves taken to maintain a coherent sense of selfhood in the face of what the person has experienced as failure in living. From a psychological point of view, it is dangerous to attack a person's faith commitment—however strange it is—when this person shows signs of discouragement in facing life tasks. You cannot be sure that such discouragement exists unless you have already noticed it. In any case, it is best not to rush into a depreciation of or attack on the person's new involvement. Given the dynamics of defiance, such an attack might push the person more firmly into a commitment to the group.

5. *Whatever you do, do not communicate to the young person that he or she is viewed as deviant or defective.* Remember that the personal identity of a young adult may still be forming. Communicating to a person that he or she is a loser because of involvement with a cult only confirms and reinforces any negative self-images and identifications. Be careful not to communicate, "You are a total disappointment. You are not really my child—any child of mine would know better than this. Anyone who would get into this has to be crazy. I am worried sick about you. I don't think you will make it through this. You are never going to get your life together." We have often seen parents communicating these messages to their children. Even though such feelings are perhaps understandable, they are extremely destructive when verbalized to a struggling young adult.

6. *Try to communicate respect, as well as confidence in the person's ability to find his or her way in life, to make decisions, and to learn from experiences.* The message the child receives through your communications should be; "You are my daughter (son). Any child of mine has resources for adapting to life. I have confidence in you. I know that whatever our differences now, we will continue to relate and love each other through the years. I recognize your right to your own opinion and your own style of living. I may not

agree with you about your current involvement, but I know it is meaningful to you. Because you are an intelligent person, you must be getting something out of it or you would leave the group. If you decide that it is not living up to your expectations, you will leave it on your own. If this time should come, I will be willing to help you explore other options. If this time does not come, we can still love each other." In short, communications should not add to the problem. The person should be affirmed, communication and options for the future left open.

7. *Do not medicalize unnecessarily*. Remember, there is little hard data on which to base the assumption that joining a group indicates psychopathology. Indeed, unless a person has a history of fairly severe psychological problems or has recently shown signs of adaptive problems, his or her joining a group does not necessarily signal a need for psychological help. If signs of psychological problems are evident, decisions as to the proper response are complex. We discuss these situations below.

8. *If the young person has had adaptive problems previously and has played the role of the problem person in the family, a family therapist should be consulted*. The first mental health professional consulted should, in most cases, be a family therapist.* Family religious conflict is a common expression of conflict based in the family system.[25] Even if there have been no previous adaptive problems, consulting a family therapist is a good idea for a number of reasons. First, individuals cannot easily assess their own family systems. A skilled outside observer can help family members understand the way in which their particular system is set up, which alliances are operative, which family member, if any, is playing the role of the "identified patient." An especially helpful aspect of family therapy in this context is that parents can say, "Father and I wanted to examine our marriage and our relationships with you

* The American Association for Marriage and Family Therapy can refer you to competent resource persons anywhere in the country. They may be reached by writing the Executive Director, AAMFT, 924 W. Ninth Street, Upland, CA 91786, or phoning (714) 981-0888.

115

children. The therapist wanted us all to be present and to offer our opinions and feelings about the family." It is easier for a young person to join the family in consulting a professional about the total family system than to respond positively to being singled out as the problem child who is the thorn in the family flesh. If you are really serious about helping your children and preserving family relationships, consultation with a family therapist is a must.

9. *Be honest with yourselves about the complexity of your feelings in this situation.* Working through the subtleties of your feelings with your pastor, pastoral counselor, or family therapist will help you differentiate between your fear for the welfare of your child, your anger at the child for disappointing you or for "rebelling," and your continuing affection and love. Until you understand and accept your own feelings you will not be effective in maintaining relatedness with your child. Dumping a mass of raw feelings on the child—whether by phone, letter, or in person—is likely to leave the child as confused as you are, and without a sense of your continued commitment to the relationship and openness of the future with regard to his or her place in the family.

10. *Remember the difficulties of initiation into adulthood, the nature of normal traumas of this transition, and the task of the family in helping the child launch out into independent functioning.* If you have not already begun to inform yourself about the complexities of this developmental process, begin to do so. Your pastor, pastoral counselor, or family therapist can suggest books and articles to read that will help you feel more oriented, less confused, more aware of the developmental terrain you and your child are traversing. Understanding the complexity of this process will make you more compassionate with yourselves as parents and with your maturing young adult. It will also make you less vulnerable to those who might want to exploit your lack of information and your desperation, as well as to those who mean well but are equally uninformed or misinformed.

11. *If you have already alienated your child by your response,*

and communication has terminated and you cannot locate your child, seek help in contacting your child and in reestablishing trust. First of all, remember that your child is at least as aware as you are of *your emotional importance to him or her*. If you have tried to intimidate, browbeat, or otherwise coerce the young adult into a change of mind and commitments, your task will be harder. If you have had the person kidnapped or otherwise forcibly detained in order to subject him or her to the deprogramming process, the problem of reestablishing trust may be a formidable one. Remember, however, that a formidable task is not necessarily an impossible one.

Do not believe anyone who suggests to you that it is impossible to locate your child or that it is always necessary to hire someone to locate a group member. Resources listed in Appendix A can help put you in touch with institutions or persons willing to help you, usually free of charge. In Berkeley, California, for example, the Berkeley Area Interfaith Council (BAIC) seeks to maintain friendly relationships with alternative religions in the area. Experienced in locating group members for families, they often set up meetings between a group member and his or her parents, if desired. According to the BAIC, groups generally insist that meetings be held at their own centers, because they fear possible kidnapping for purposes of deprogramming. A private room is usually provided for member and visitors to talk. If parents are uncomfortable going to such a center alone, BAIC will arrange for an appropriate religious leader—Protestant, Catholic, or Jewish—to accompany them.

12. *If you have been able to locate the group member but fear getting back into destructive and alienating patterns of communication, seek out a mediator.* Here again, the BAIC offers a good model. BAIC has a list of volunteers who, unlike deprogrammers, refuse to take sides in the family religious conflict but envision their role as that of facilitating "frank and respectful sharing and mutual understanding."

13. *When your child remains in a group but comes home for*

a *visit, act as naturally as possible.* Most important, do not act as if a flying saucer has landed in your yard and an alien has appeared in your living room! This is your child. No matter how strange she or he dresses or what odd philosophy she or he espouses, do not act as if you are in the presence of a weirdo. Keep your mind on the struggle your child is engaged in as she or he seeks to emerge as an adult from the family. Be as honest as you can without being hostile or unnecessarily confrontive. If you cannot be civil when discussing religious matters, then "negotiate" a truce in this area of life and put your energies into telling the group member about what has been happening in the family since her or his absence. Until you are told otherwise, *assume* your child is interested. One caution: Do not go into a litany of praise for the sibling or siblings who play the role(s) of "golden boy" and "golden girl" in the family. Such implicit and unfavorable comparisons may be partly the reason why the young person is in the group. Facts can and should be reported but without adulatory embellishment. If the person wishes to relate accounts of events, activities, and so on within the group, be good listeners without constantly injecting depreciatory comments. If you are asked what you think about the story that has been related, give an honest but not hostile response. You can honestly claim lack of sufficient information and understanding to make any sweeping statements, and therefore, you are in a good position to ask questions that may give you insight into the person's experience of life in the group.

Act and speak in ways that communicate "You are still part of this family." Do not guilt-trip the person with lines like: "Grandmother is just killed that you dropped out of college and joined this cult." You can, however, communicate that the family, while recognizing and respecting his or her rights as an adult, expects to have a relationship with the young person over the coming years— whether or not he or she remains in the group.

14. *Be prepared to respond positively should your child suddenly decide to leave the group.* This is extremely important, because the majority of group members do leave of their own accord. That parents would not automatically know how to respond may

seem strange to some. Nevertheless, many parents experience their children's return as an unexpected and confusing new development. In part, they experience a joyous welcome; in part, they question, "Now what do we do?"

First, the former group member probably has sufficient questions about his or her time spent in the alternative religion and enough self-doubt in beginning again with the previous home as a base of operations that he or she does not need to have any "I told you so's" communicated. To support a view of the time spent in the group as a meaningful experience, understandable in the context of their developmental journey, is more constructive and encouraging. Any parental depreciation of the significance of the experience lends credence to the young person's tendencies to view himself or herself as a damaged or defective personality.

Second, if no family therapy has been initiated, this is a natural time to examine family patterns that may have made it difficult for this child in particular. The problem has not been solved with the return of the group member. The developmental task of individuation from the family still must be faced—and the person may be more discouraged than before.

Third, do not be afraid or embarrassed to offer your adult offspring assistance—financial and otherwise—during this transitional time. Many parents consider it inappropriate to give financial support to an adult child not still in school. Those who do give such support usually feel ashamed and embarrassed to admit it. Such aid, however, is appropriate in transitional situations. It should be made clear that the assistance is not unlimited—not a carte blanche—but is intended to facilitate their reentry into life outside the group.

Fourth, as soon as possible, help the young person move out of your home. The experiment with living out of the family residence needs to continue, even if this necessitates a temporary subsidy by parents. If financial or other circumstances make it necessary for the son or daughter to live with his or her parents, then ground rules appropriate for an *adult* boarder should be negotiated. This is usually difficult, especially for parents, and arrangements for living with another family member may prove to be more satisfactory.

119

Many times uncles, aunts, grandparents, and other extended family members do a better job of encouraging young adults to face the world than their own parents. Where a real aunt or uncle is not available, a close family friend can serve as a surrogate uncle (or aunt) and can be helpful in supporting and encouraging the young person as he or she begins to work again on the initiation into adulthood. Often a therapeutic relationship with a pastoral counselor, family therapist, or other mental health professional can be encouraged at this time with good results. Sometimes a young person tells his or her parents, "I'll go if you will." If they say this, *quickly* take them up on it. Everyone will benefit.

Finally, get your unrealistic expectations under control. These days it is especially hard for young adults to establish themselves in the world. Expectations are high, especially in middle-class or upper-middle-class families. The suicide rate among adolescents and young adults from successful, upper-middle-class families attests to the discouraging impact of having successful parents to try to live up to. Economic and other realities make it more difficult for a young person to "make it" today than during the fifties and sixties era of growth and expansion in so many fields. *It is important for you to learn to celebrate small victories.* A series of small victories is the only durable way toward maturation, and the encouraging parent learns to become an expert at noticing small but significant progress and helping the young person claim and celebrate it.

15. *If your child has been in a group for a long time and shows no sign of leaving, continue to seek an improved and mutually respectful relationship with your child.* If, for example, your child shows signs of becoming a lifelong Hindu or Buddhist monk, you must get clear as to your point of view about the rights of an adult to practice his or her religion of choice in America. Such rights must be respected; coercive methods of deconversion should not be tolerated in a democratic society. If you maintain or reestablish communication with your child and assure him or her of continued love and support from the family, should he or she become disillusioned with the group, a return home will be easier to face. If the young person decides to remain in the group, you will be able to

maintain and enhance family relationships across the boundaries of the religious differences involved. Adult children should have the right to live their own lives, to make their own philosophical and value choices, *even if their parents believe these choices are dangerous, impractical, or otherwise misguided.* The young adult should not be expected to purchase the love and continued relationship with the family at the price of freedom and integrity.

16. *If you believe your child has major emotional problems, perhaps involving a severe mental illness, carefully evaluate both your reasons for coming to this conclusion and the resources and alternatives available to assist your child.* First, make sure that you are not using faulty reasoning which leads to the conclusion that group membership itself is a diagnostic indicator. If your judgment is based on maladaptive behaviors that antedated the beginning of group membership—previous hospitalizations, previous psychiatric care, or the like—you are correct to be concerned that the basic adaptive difficulties may continue to be a problem for the group member. Again, you should investigate the possibility that the acting out of the young person may have been related to the structures of the family system and not to major intrapsychic problems. Consultation with a family therapist can help clarify the situation. Second, group membership may have been therapeutic, assisting the young person to resolve some of the problems he or she brought along into the group. Sometimes groups press members to seek therapy from secular therapists to assist them in resolving problems that have become evident in the course of group life.

Nevertheless, the very real possibility remains that your young adult may still be suffering from a severe psychological disorder. Let us assume this is the case. Immediately take stock with regard to resources, possible lines of influence, and alternatives. We do not favor deprogramming in any situation and suggest that in cases like this, deprogramming is contraindicated for psychological reasons. Contact with the young person should be maintained or reestablished, if possible. A mediator may facilitate not only an opportunity to express your love and concern to the child, but also a chance to enlist the cooperation of leaders of the alternative group

121

in getting appropriate medical assistance for the group member. Certain mental health professionals are trusted by the leadership of alternative religions and might be part of a meeting arranged through a mediator.

Before deciding to have the person hospitalized, either through some coercive tactic or by achieving his or her consent through persuasion, be sure such a decision is warranted. Get more than one opinion. Remember that hospitalizations now tend to be rather brief and to utilize drug therapy rather than psychotherapy. When the hospitalization ends will you be able to provide the young person with an environment as humane and supportive as he or she had in the religious community? Few families have the financial resources to keep their adult children in the kind of high-quality residential treatment center that offers both therapy and differing degrees of independence as treatment progresses. If after hospitalization an attempt is made to continue therapy on an outpatient basis, the question of living arrangements, the development of meaningful relationships and activities, again becomes focal. To provide a living situation for your troubled son or daughter that offers as humane a living situation as life in many of the alternative religious groups will be difficult, if not impossible. Remember, the mainline denominations currently offer little help in this area and government budget cuts have crippled many public attempts to provide such facilities for chronically troubled persons.

If you find that hospitalization would not be an improvement and that you cannot get your group member into therapy at this time, there is still hope. Continue to put your energies into repairing and enhancing communication. Your improved relationship may enable you to help your child get the help he or she needs. Maintained communication and rebuilding of relationship are your best hopes. Find a mental health professional who has experience in such situations to serve as your consultant. Such a person can help you to understand ways in which to minimize destructive aspects of the relationship. Greater knowledge of yourself may, in fact, have a liberating effect on your adult child. In any case, you will have the satisfaction of knowing that you are doing all you can to offer your child the possibility of a healing therapeutic relationship, if not now, then perhaps in future months or years. In the meantime an improved relationship with you will remove much of the stress open family warfare puts on a child. Your child will be happier and better able to put his or her energies into the adaptive tasks confronted daily in group life.

17. *Remember that membership in an alternative religion may not indicate a child is brainwashed, mentally ill, or the victim of destructive family dynamics.* In fact, a healthy family that models independent functioning and decision-making, that values transpersonal moral and religious ideals, might give a young person courage to experiment with the unfamiliar, to break with the ego mass of the family and march to his or her own drummer. Normally, the young person must be very healthy to explore the unknown as a "stranger in a strange land," taking risks in moving out of ethnic, familial, or ideological enclaves. *We must emphasize again that there is no conclusive evidence which establishes that membership in an alternative religion is diagnostic for personal or family pathology.* Pathology in the member's personality or in his or her family of origin *may* be present, but this must be determined on the basis of individual cases, just as one would do in the case of Jews or Episcopalians.

18. *Accept the fact that a normal healthy child of a normal healthy family may spend his or her life as a member of an alternative religion.* In the context of the new religious pluralism we find an increasing number of cases in which this is true. As religious leaders and families committed to a particular tradition, we want to be as faithful and effective as possible in representing and stewarding this tradition, but we must realize that we cannot, indeed *should not*, impose fidelity to this tradition on our children through coercion of any kind. To attempt to do so or to support attempts to do so would be to join the cultural regression to a premodern authoritarianism that appears so attractive to many at this time. *We must therefore be prepared to allow our adult children to be adults, to be independent, to be different, even to be wrong, without losing our love and basic respect.*[26]

APPENDIX A

A BRIEF GUIDE TO THE MAJOR
ALTERNATIVE RELIGIONS

More than 600 religious groups in the United States and in Canada could properly be termed alternative religions. Most are so small that the likelihood of meeting a member is slight. Others have made homes for themselves on the religious landscape and could almost be considered accepted; Christian Science is such a group. Many alternative religions serve particular ethnic groups and are not seen by people outside these ethnic communities.

Of the 600 groups, approximately 75 have been identified as cults by modern anti-cultists. These groups are identified mainly by their reception of a large percentage of their members from among the young white, middle-class population of the 1970s. Many are in their first generation of existence in North America. The largest of these groups number less than 10,000, and the two most famous—the Hare Krishna and the Unification Church—number less than 5,000. On the average these groups have 1,000 to 3,000 members. Thus, an estimated 150,000 individuals are involved in the so-called cults at any one time. Each of these groups experiences a large overturn In membership.

Reports of cults numbering in the thousands and involving

people in the millions contain grossly exaggerated figures circulated by anti-cult groups to promote a climate of hysteria. Such figures have no basis in fact and represent, at best, the wild speculations of those who make their living fighting alternative religions.

Of the 75 cults, almost all attention has been focused on 13 alternative religions:

The Church of Armageddon
The Church Universal and Triumphant
The Church of Scientology
The International Society for Krishna Consciousness
    (Hare Krishna)
Transcendental Meditation
Divine Light Mission
Zen Buddhism
Nichiren Shoshu of America (Soka Gakkai)
The Children of God/Family of Love
The Christian Foundation
The Local Church
Way International
The Unification Church

Besides these thirteen groups we have added consideration of two groups rarely encountered by anti-cultists but which nevertheless have made an impact on the cult problem because of the general cultural fear of them—Witchcraft and Satanism. These groups are discussed under five headings: communal, psychic, magical, eastern, and Christian.

This guide attempts to introduce each group through its history and teachings,with the goal of providing a start at understanding the group's peculiarities. Where possible, a further source for more in-depth study is cited. Often this source is a publication distributed by the group or one authored by a sympathetic outsider. One should encounter the group on its own terms before formulating a criticism. We also note that most books written about cults are hostile to the groups and highly inaccurate in reporting their beliefs and practices. Such books are more interested in refuting the groups than in giving readers any understanding of them.[1]

COMMUNAL GROUPS

All the great religious traditions have made a place for people who wish to live a strong communal existence built on the mutual sharing and consumption of the individual's resources. Many religious groups, including Christianity, were founded as communal groups. The Christian ideal of communal living spelled out in the book of Acts has continually inspired groups in the West during the past 2,000 years. Many of the communal groups that survive into a second generation abandon communal living. The Mormons, originally organized into the United Society, abandoned communal living in the 1840s and have since been plagued by schismatic groups that wish to reinstitute what they consider an essential of Mormon faith.

America has had two main periods in which numerous communes were formed. The first occurred in the 1840s; the second in the 1960s. Successful communes, a small minority of the whole, survive the first winter and continue for many years; a few survive into the second and third generations. Those that survive do so because of a strong organization that can stave off the continual lure of the world to abandon their peculiar ways. Thus, the successful commune generally has a strong (often autocratic) leadership and a strong ethos—usually a particular religion—that serve both to separate the group from the world and to bind the members of the group closely together. Too much interaction with nonmembers, especially with persons to whom members might have emotional ties, is highly destructive of communal existence. Communal groups adopt mechanisms to prevent illicit intercourse with the world. They change their names, develop in-group jargon and rituals, and hold secrets. Commonly included in their private world are practices that have a clear logic and/or rationale within the context but which, when looked on by an outsider, can appear sinister, psychotic, or just plain weird.

Sex is a powerful force that, if uncontrolled, can destroy a communal group quickly. Communal groups usually adopt one of two patterns: abstinence or group marriage. In the former, a pattern of the Hare Krishna, sexual feelings are sublimated and directed to

127

communal symbols; in the Hare Krishna's case, the deities. Other groups—the Oneida Community being the most famous—adopt a pattern in which sexual activity is diffused through the community; thus no particular infatuation can replace the group as the first concern of any individual.

THE CHURCH OF ARMAGEDDON

This group became famous when a major network filmed an attempted deprogramming by Ted Patrick of one of its members. Then the press discovered that Steve Allen's son was a leading member. The Church was founded in 1969 by Paul Erdmann in Seattle, Washington.

The communal organization of the Church of Armageddon takes the form of an extended family, and each member takes the family name Israel. As a first name they take the name of a virtue or attribute—love, serious, contemplation, etc. Paul Erdmann, the leader, is known as Love Israel, and the group is frequently referred to as the Love Israel Family.

On joining, members give up their earthly goods to the group and renounce the world. In particular, they renounce the worldly traditions of matrimony. As with Christian monastics, they see themselves both collectively and individually as married to Christ. Members also see themselves as married to one another, with the men as husbands having authority over the women as wives. In practice, their relationship is as brothers and sisters. The leaders of the Church have the authority to allow individual "bonding" for the purpose of having children.

A book written by Love Israel entitled *Love* serves as the standard of teaching for the group. The Church of Armageddon is the continuation of Israel (Old Testament) and follows the primitive teachings of Jesus Christ (New Testament). Eating and drinking are sacramental; whatever is eaten is the body of Christ, and whatever is drunk, his blood. When one joins he or she is freed from the past life in the world of sin and death. Baptism by immersion is practiced.

Headquarters of the Church is in a residential section of Seattle.

128

Outposts of the community in Hawaii and Alaska were recently closed. There are appoximately 400 members.

The Church has been accused of violent activity, but as yet no evidence of such activity has been presented. Much of the substance of the accusation derived from the death in 1972 of two members who took an overdose of toluene, a solvent that alters the state of consciousness when inhaled and that was used in a religious rite. This group was also accused of trying to take over Queen Anne Hill, the section of Seattle its original commune is located in, but time has proved the charge to be empt speculation. Members live a clannish existence and have cut themselves off from many worldly pursuits.

PSYCHIC GROUPS

During the 20th century the development of parapsychology into a widely recognized scientific endeavor has encouraged the growth of many groups that base their beliefs around psychic-occult phenomena. Such groups, including the Spiritualists and Theosophists, were among the original groups labeled cults early in this century. Spiritualism and Theosophy have been around for more than a century and have a membership that reflects their maturity. Although neither benefited greatly from the influx of young adults into alternative religions in the 1970s, some basic understanding of each will help in understanding one of the major groups labeled cult—the Church Universal and Triumphant.

A basic belief of Spiritualism is that certain people, called mediums, can through trance or just clear psychic perception contact entities of the spirit world. In classic Spiritualism the primary entities mediums attempted to contact were the recently deceased relatives of persons who attended the seances—meetings whose purpose was spirit contact. Spiritualists believed that, along with the dead, they frequently contacted other entities, highly evolved spirits, from whom they could learn of the true nature of life and of the life to come. Out of classic Spiritualism arose a form of teaching Spiritualism in which the major activity consisted of learning about spiritual life from spirit teachers.

129

Theosophy grew out of Spiritualism. Madame Helena Petrovna Blavatsky, Theosophy's main teacher and leader, claimed contact with a series of evolved beings, whom she called mahatmas or masters. Some of these beings were spirits; some were reincarnated in bodies. Together, the masters formed a spiritual hierarchy between humans and the divine, with Madame Blavatsky as their spokesperson. The hierarchy governed the world and controlled the various spheres of human existence.

Closest to humanity and in direct contact with Madame Blavatsky were the Lords of the Seven Rays. In occult terms the basic areas of human life, such as beauty, science, devotion, and service, were associated with the seven colors of the light spectrum. Light itself is, of course, the most characteristic manifestation of the divine. When light comes to a person this person intuitively perceives truth. When a particularly colored light comes to someone he or she perceives the truth in one area of existence.

During her life Madame Blavatsky was the main person in contact with the masters. After her death the leaders of the Theosophical Society frowned on anyone who attempted to replace her as the regular go-between with the masters. Some who tried, such as Alice Bailey, were eased out of the group.

Among those who claimed to have come in contact with the masters, Guy Ballard (AKA Godfre Ray King) established his own competing group—the Great I AM—in Chicago in the 1930s. After his death, during World War II, his wife succeeded him and led the group until her death, in the late 1970s.

Over the past several decades the I AM splintered into a number of groups—The Bridge to Freedom, the Ascended Master Fellowship, and the Sanctuary of the Master's Presence. Of these various splinters the only one to attain anything similar to the success of the original I AM group has been the Summit Lighthouse, better known by the name it adopted in the 1970s: the Church Universal and Triumphant.

THE CHURCH UNIVERSAL AND TRIUMPHANT

The Church Universal and Triumphant was founded as the Summit Lighthouse in 1958 by Mark and Elizabeth Clare Prophet, two former members of the Bridge to Freedom, the original I AM splinter. For many years the group was headquartered in Colorado Springs but moved to Pasadena in the midseventies, after Mark's death in 1973, and then to its present location near Malibu, California, site of a former Roman Catholic college. During the 1970s the present name gradually replaced the original one.

The Church has a sophisticated theology drawn from Theosophy and centered on the Prophets' roles as communication links with the Ascended Masters. Since his death Mark has been considered one of the Lords of the Seven Rays. At present Elizabeth Prophet is the special messenger of the spiritual hierarchy, especially of one master, El Morya. During many of the gatherings at which Ms. Prophet presides a communication from one or more of the masters to those gathered is the main event.

The Church also follows the practice of decreeing, a form of spiritual exercise developed by Guy Ballard. Decrees are short statements of one's wishes for the self or the world stated in such a way that the words demand the divine to act on these wishes. Such decrees are repeated in a loud voice and a chanting rhythm.

During the 1970s a distinct change took place in the Church. In its early years the Summit Lighthouse related to members primarily through the mail. Members received periodicals and lessons from the Colorado Springs headquarters and gathered in the summer for conferences. In the late 1970s Ms. Prophet, now styled as Guru Ma, borrowing an image from many of the Eastern teachers, began to evangelize among young adults and to build groups of followers, congregations, around the country. To further expand its outreach to the public the Church increased the number of books and written materials it produced and created several sets of tapes.

During the several decades of its existence, primarily through its mail courses, the Church has built a large following, numbering in the thousands in the United States and with an additional significant following in West Africa (Ghana and Liberia).

The main criticism of the Church Universal and Triumphant, besides the usual brainwashing claims, derives from the group's manifest prosperity, as evidenced, for example, by the purchase of the college campus in California (renamed Camelot), the slick publications, and the tuition charges at Summit University (the Church's school). Although the figures may seem large and like any sizable religious organization the Church has a large cash flow, no evidence of improper use or accumulation of money has been presented, even though several high-level members of the group have left it.

(Most accusations against religious organizations for having a money orientation or a great deal of wealth are made apart from any analysis of what happens to the money a religious group takes in, how this money compares to the money taken in by more established churches and synagogues, and how much money it takes to operate a religious institution, such as a school. Apart from such comparable figures, reflections on a particular group's high cash flow hides an unstated and unproven accusation that the leader(s) are hoarding the wealth and getting rich at the expense of gullible followers.

The accusation of a religon's existing only to accumulate money for the benefit of a few is as old as religion itself. And on occasion religion has been undeniably so used. But apart from evidence that, in fact, a few are growing wealthy from the givings of the members, claims—covert or overt—based merely on the calculated cash flow of a group become empty. Evidence that a few are growing wealthy would be grounds for the removal of their tax exempt status by the Internal Revenue Service.)

THE CHURCH OF SCIENTOLOGY

The Church of Scientology was founded in 1955 by L. Ron Hubbard. During his earlier years Hubbard served as an officer in the U.S. Navy, operated as an investigator for the Los Angeles Police Department, authored fiction and nonfiction books, and became an accomplished amateur philosopher. His philosophical and theological speculations led to his development of a practical system for human improvement, which he termed Dianetics. Scientology is the natural extension of Dianetics into a total philosophical and theological teaching and program.

The Church's belief is quite eclectic. Hubbard draws ideas

from both Eastern and Ancient Greek thought as well as from modern occultism and individualism. The Church teaches that humans are basically good and ever strive to survive. Each person is designated a Thetan, i.e., a soul, an individual force. The Thetan controls the body and is the essence of the responsible self. The incarnated Thetan is hindered from full ability to express goodness and survive by painful past experiences. The attainment of self-knowledge allows the individual to increase his or her ability to survive and express the good innate within the self.

The Church's activities all aim at increasing self-knowledge. The Scientologist begins his or her work on the mind, which has stored all experiences, including mental image pictures of past experiences of pain and negativity (engrams). Engrams are kept in what is called the Reactive mind. When unconsciously released they impose themselves on the person. When consciously released they can be erased and denied their power.

A special pastoral counseling process called auditing is used to assist individuals to remove engrams. Once clear, the Scientologist can begin to develop the potentials of the Thetan, which includes the ability to free itself from the body for short periods.

No church has been involved in so much controversy as has the Church of Scientology, with the possible exception of the Unification Church. It has since its founding been almost continuously in court on a variety of issues ranging from suing the Food and Drug Administration to defending itself against charges of stealing from the government. It took to task for libel authors who wrote about the Church, and it usually won. For more than a decade it has battled with the Internal Revenue Service about its tax exemption.

Of all the religious groups in America the Church of Scientology is the most difficult to evaluate. It has made enemies who will go far out of their way—and have—to see it destroyed. It fights just as tenaciously to defend itself at all costs. For more than 20 years it has been involved in a growing war with the anti-cult movement and the government. So complex has this situation become that only when the dust settles from the various court cases still in progress will a full understanding be possible.

Certain facts lead one to tentative conclusions. First, the conviction of Scientology leaders in the recent case of theft of government property has demonstrated that overzealous Scientologists have gone to great extremes—even to the point of committing a felony—to defend the Church. The same case also proved that the Church has been continually lied to by government agencies. The release of reams of secret Scientology files, while containing some evidence of highly questionable behavior on the Church's part—such as the collection of dossiers on Church "enemies"—also failed to reveal that the Church was engaged in widespread nefarious plots.

Interestingly, the controversies in which this church has been involved have all centered on the Guardian's Office, a special division of the Church set up to defend the Church against what it felt were unjustified attacks and slander. While the rest of the Church carried out its program, individuals in the Guardian's Office had a great deal of freedom to carry out actions they felt were necessary to defend the Church against its enemies. In 1981 the Church announced a wholesale replacement of leaders in this office.

Thus, the final word on the Church of Scientology must wait. Meanwhile, the Church has remained most open to inquiries by interested individuals who wish to know the Church's position on the many charges that have been leveled against it.[2]

MAGICAL GROUPS

Few words in the cult realms stir emotions as much as Witchcraft and Satanism. The two have been locked together at least since the Middle Ages, and both began a comeback in the 1960s. Although neither has received the attention of anti-cultists that some of the more public groups have, in the interface between parents and sons and daughters involved in an alternative religion, Witchcraft is more likely to appear than any group in this guide. There are approximately 30,000 to 40,000 Witches and Neo-Pagans, collectively three times as many participants as the most successful of the better known cults.

To understand Witchcraft and Satanism it is necessary to distinguish them. Whatever might have been their connection in centuries past, today they are distinct phenomena. Satanism is the worship of the Christian personification of evil. Even though it is a rare phenomenon, it has been known periodically to make an appearance in Western culture. Witchcraft, at least as practiced today, is a revival of ancient pagan fertility religion believed by its adherents to have been the dominant pre-Christian religion of Europe. Its main deities are the Great Mother Goddess and the Horned God—Diana and Pan—derived from Greek mythology. Although there are many thousands of Neo-Pagans, there have never been more than 2,000 or 3,000 Satanists and that was in the early seventies, at the height of the popularity of Anton LeVey's Church of Satan.

Thus, to interact correctly in a situation where one party is self-identified as a Witch, it is important for all concerned to dismiss notions that the Witch is involved in bloody rituals, rites parodying Christian worship, and malevolent magic.

WITCHCRAFT

Witchcraft, as practiced today, began in England in the 1940s. It was created (or revived) by Gerald Gardner, a retired British civil servant. While serving in southern Asia he had become attracted to magic and to the worship of the Mother Goddess. Once back in England he formed a coven, the basic organizational grouping in the Craft, and promulgated his teachings. He wrote a set of rituals that have become widely circulated, and following Gardner's lead others produced materials also.

After Gardner's books were published, in the 1950s, people flocked to him for initiation into Witchcraft, and almost all present-day Neo-Pagan groups derive from his efforts. In the mid-1960s, several Americans—including Ray and Rosemary Buckland, and Donna Cole—traveled to England and brought back Gardner's teaching.

Witchcraft has two foci—magic and the Goddess. Magic is the art of causing change by an act of the will, using cosmic magical power. Witches use magical power mainly for high magic, changing the individual self into a perfected human. It can also be used for

135

low, or mundane magic, making change in the visible world. The major uses are to heal and to assist a member of the coven to attain something, such as a new job. A moral principle, the Wiccan Rede— "Except ye harm none, do what thou wilt"—controls the use of magic, and except on rare occasions, curses against someone would not be used.

Witches worship the Earth Mother, although they call Her by many names, depending on which ancient form of Pagan thought attracts them. The setting of the Mother Goddess and the Horned God as the leading deities of Witchcraft sets Witches in search of a balanced life. They seek balance between inner-outer, male-female, passive-aggressive, and spiritual-material.

Witches are organized into small groups (usually five to fifteen people) called covens, although some Neo-Pagan groups call them groves or nests. These are autonomous groups that normally gather biweekly, on the full and new moons (esbats), and annually on eight major festivals (called sabbats). Worship is conducted inside a circle, the visible sign of a sphere imagined to surround the coven when it meets. In the basic ritual act, called "drawing down the moon," psychic energy is pictured as being raised in a cone over the coven and then pulled into the circle.

Witches do not recruit, and new members have to be self-motivated enough either to find a group or locate the books necessary to start a group of their own. Within the movement are a number of "solitaries," who work the Craft as a personal spiritual path without the more elaborate rituals of the group.[3]

SATANISM

Satanism, the worship of the Christian personification of evil, was revived in the mid-1960s by Anton LeVey, who founded the Church of Satan on April, 30, 1966. For the Church, Satan is identified as Lucifer, the light-bearer, the principle of nature at its highest. Satan is also identified with the snake in the Garden of Eden, who destroyed innocence by bringing knowledge.

Satanists see themselves as developing the self to the fullest and upholding personal values as opposed to altruistic virtues. Because the self is the highest embodiment of life it is sacred, and indulgence and vital existence are proper modes of being.

As spread in the 1970s, Satanism manifested itself basically as a movement teaching self-assertion. It was not involved in animal sacrifice or acts of violence against individuals. These rare actions can be found as part of informal groups where psychopathology is present.

Because of the very nature of Satanism—either in its tamer aspect in teaching self-assertion or its more pathological one—it is a short-lived phenomenon and rarely involves individuals for more than a few years.

EASTERN GROUPS

Eastern religion has been present in the United States since the late 19th century but until the mid-1960s was largely confined to Asian-American communities, intellectuals, and a few socialites. Then, in 1965, the Oriental Exclusion Acts were repealed, and large-scale immigration began from India and was revived from Japan. Along with the immigrants came religious leaders—gurus (teachers) and swamis (monks). While making good newspaper copy because their dress and behavior differ from that of Western priests and preachers, in Eastern society they occupy the same positions as do the religious functionaries that are more familiar to Americans. They come as both religious leaders of immigrant communities and as missionaries of Eastern religions.

Within Eastern religion the basic leader is a guru, or sensei (literally: teacher). Typically, the guru teaches the student (chela) a set of spiritual techniques, which the student practices to attain spiritual goals. The guru is also seen as an embodiment of the spiritual goals and attainment of them is the source of the guru's authority. Thus, an accomplished yogi has the authority to teach yoga. The techniques of spiritual discipline vary widely. Yoga, for example, may take the form of hatha (postures), karma (work), bhakti (devotion), japa (repeating mantras), raja (meditation), or tantra (sex). Meditation is the most popular spiritual discipline, but among different groups the form of meditation varies tremendously.

Almost all the Eastern groups currently functioning in the United States were founded by a single teacher, who gathered a small group of disciples around him and then spread as opportunity allowed. Following Eastern patterns, all spiritual authority is invested in the guru, who passes it on to others as the group requires. When a leader dies, this person is succeeded by someone previously appointed to be the leader's successor, a new leader elected by the group in some way, or a collective leadership. Also, as the group grows and spreads into a national movement, it must shift from reliance on personal contact with and instruction from the leader and place increased reliance on more impersonal methods of contact through printed instructional materials.

The basic problem of alternative religion—how to integrate new members—is most obvious in the Eastern religions. Because the average convert knows little of Eastern religion the new member must be put through a concentrated educational process during the first few years of membership. This process, which takes the place of the learning a person raised in a Hindu or Buddhist society would normally receive during the childhood and teen years, is so intense because instead of just learning a few differences, as when a Methodist becomes a Presbyterian, the average new member must learn a whole new way to be religious.

INTERNATIONAL SOCIETY FOR KRISHNA CONSCIOUSNESS (HARE KRISHNA)

Second only to the Unification Church as a focus of the cult controversy, the Hare Krishna movement was founded in 1965 by A.C. Bhaktivedanta Swami Prabhupada, an independent teacher out of the Chaitanya tradition of Bengal. Lord Chaitanya Mahaprabhu (1486-1534), a contemporary of Martin Luther, led a bhakti-yoga reform movement within 16th-century Hinduism.

The Society takes its teachings from the *Bhagavad Gita,* one of several sacred Hindu books, and worships Krishna as the eternal, omniscient, omnipresent, omnipotent, and all-attractive Personality of Godhead. All actions are performed as acts of devotion to Krishna; for example, all food is offered to Krishna before it is eaten.

The main act of devotion is the repetition of the Hare Krishna mantra. The chanting of the words

> Hare Krishna, Hare Krishna
> Hare Hare Krishna Krishna
> Hare Rama, Hare Rama
> Hare Hare Rama Rama

is seen as the best method in this day and age of receiving the pure consciousness of God (in his incarnations of Krishna and Rama) and dispelling the maya (illusion) in which we are all immersed. The Society promotes the frequent recital of the mantra among its members as well as people in general.

The movement is organized on a noncloistered monastic model. Partly because of the demands of its ascetic life-style, the Society has not grown beyond a few thousand members, who rise early each day and follow a scheduled routine. A typical day includes a ritual bath, the marking of the body with clay (telok), service to the deity statues, public chanting of the Hare Krishna mantra (kirtan), and study of the Gita and related materials.

Because of the demands of the life of a Krishna member, devotees do little recruiting. Most new members are people who have heard of the movement and who come to a temple and ask to join. Usually they are either familiar with and inclined toward Eastern religion and/or are vegetarians. They are then put through a period of training to test their resolve and acceptability.

The main source of tension between Krishna devotees and their critics derives from the purity code. Devotees attempt to separate themselves from the world of illusion. They symbolize this separation by taking a ritual bath daily, abstaining from regular company with non-Krishnas, eating only prasadam (food offered to Krishna), taking a new name, and avoiding the reading of too many non-Krishna books. Avoiding contact with non-Krishnas can take the form of a devotee losing contact with his or her immediate family.

Krishnas have received negative criticism for their fund-raising in airports and other public facilities, and steps have been taken to limit their contact with passengers. Recently, wide media coverage was given to accusations that Krishnas were stockpiling weapons, after several weapons had been found in a member's automobile. Unfortunately, little coverage was given to a later announcement that no substance to the charge was discovered and that the Society, which is pacifist as a matter of basic teaching, had previously instructed the said member to get rid of his weapons. Although new members are still taken in, growth of the Society has slowed, and membership seems to have leveled out at around 3,000. Where temples are located a large group of nonmembers may gather on Sundays, when the Krishnas give their free feasts.[4]

TRANSCENDENTAL MEDITATION

Transcendental Meditation (TM) is a yoga discipline featured in the teachings of an organization called the World Plan Executive Council. The corporate name refers to the plan for spreading the teachings of Maharishi Mahesh Yogi, its guru. The Maharishi came out of 13 years of seclusion with his teacher, Guru Dev, in 1958 and began spreading his teachings, which gained early notoriety when the Beatles, Mia Farrow, and Jane Fonda became TM practitioners.

The Council consists of five task-oriented structures. The International Meditation Society is the main structure to introduce TM to the general public. The Student International Meditation Society introduces TM to the student population. Maharishi International University is a regular four-year university that offers both bachelor's and master's degrees. The university, formerly Parson's College in Fairfield, Iowa, has shaped its curriculum on TM principles. The American Foundation for the Science of Creative Intelligence is working to introduce TM principles into the business community. Finally, the Spiritual Regeneration Movement works with the older generation, i.e., those over 30.

TM is a form of japa-yoga—meditation with a mantra. Unlike the Hare Krishna practice, the usual TM mantra consists of one or two words that are repeated silently and on which the meditator concentrates. The practice of TM allows the practitioner to contact the absolute field of pure being—unmanifested and transcendental. This being is the ultimate reality of creation. Once meditation begins, the individual also begins to "live the being," and the Maharishi offers instruction on correct thinking, speaking, action, behavior, and health. The goal is God-realization. The Maharishi's teaching is the summation of the practical wisdom of the integrated life as advanced by the Vedic Rishis of Ancient India; that is, TM proposes to reach the spiritual goals of humanity in this generation.

TM had a spectacular growth during the 1970s. Almost a million people took the basic TM course, then, at the end of the decade, the number of new meditators dropped markedly and the organization suffered some dramatic reverses, occasioned partly by its unique position on the question of religion.

Hindus frequently claim that Hinduism is religion itself, whereas other religions are merely limited expressions of religion, i.e., a religion. TM has gone one step farther and declared itself not a religion. It states that TM is a technique that both the religious and the nonreligious can practice. The teachings are not theology, but the science of creative intelligence. Before the court decided in 1978 that, according to American legal usage, TM constituted a religion, the practice had penetrated many public institutions, and TM instructors were being supported by schools and the armed forces. This court decision constituted a major reversal for the World Plan Executive Council.

Then the Council announced that they had successfully taught TM practitioners to levitate. The Maharishi was immediately attacked by other Hindu teachers for misrepresenting Yoga. The press called on him to put up or shut up. In both instances his credibility was severely questioned. The growth of the seventies has slowed markedly, but TM centers can still be found in most U.S. cities.[5]

DIVINE LIGHT MISSION

The Divine Light Mission was founded in India in 1960 by Sri Hans Ji Maharaj, a former member of the Radhasoami Satsang Beas.

141

The Radhasoami is one of several neo-Sikh groups, each of which is headed by a leader considered by the members to be a perfect master, or satguru. The satguru's task is to teach members the path back to God and actively to lead them as they follow the path. Soon after founding the Mission, Sri Hans Ji died and was succeeded by his youngest son, then only eight years old. At the funeral, the son is reported to have addressed the assembled crowd, "Oh, you have been illusioned by maya (the delusion that suffering is real). Maharaj Ji is here, very much present amidst you. Recognize him, adore him, and obey him."

According to the tradition of the Mission, the young guru had been an unusual child, who began meditating at age two and was giving discourses to disciples at age six. In 1970, four years after taking leadership of the Mission, Guru Maharaj Ji proclaimed the dawn of a new era and began the international expansion that brought him to the United States the next year.

Maharaj Ji initiates followers (called premies, i.e., lovers of God) through the giving of knowledge. This process involves the instruction in four yoga techniques, which the premies practice daily as a means to realize their goals of spiritual enlightenment. The first technique involves the placing of the knuckles on the eyes, an action that produces flashes of light in the head (by producing pressure on the optic nerve). The second involves the plugging of the ears and concentrating on the inner sounds. The third involves concentrating on the sound of one's own breathing. Finally, the "nectar" is a technique in which the tongue is curled backward against the roof of the mouth.

The Divine Light Mission grew quickly in the early seventies but suffered a severe setback in 1973, when a large, expensive event in the Houston Astrodome proved a major disaster, financially and otherwise. In the late seventies the Mission became a low-key organization and stopped its attempts at mass appeal. Recently, Maharaj Ji quietly moved to Miami. The Mission has reportedly initiated over 50,000 people, but only a few thousand remain in the chain of ashrams that now dot the nation.[6]

ZEN BUDDHISM

Buddhism began its spread from ethnic confines several decades before Hinduism partly because of the encounter of American soldiers with Japanese Buddhism during the occupation after World War II. The first form of Buddhism to attract attention, Zen Buddhism became an integral part of the Beat Generation in the early 1950s.

Zen is a mystical form of Buddhism that stands in relation to Buddhism as a whole much as contemplative Catholicism does to Christianity. It was begun by Bodhidharma (d. 534) and has been passed along through a lineage of "enlightened" Zen masters. Along the way Zen divided into two major schools: Rinzai and Soto. Rinzai Zen uses a practice called the koan, which is an anecdotal event or utterance given to a student as a problem. Mastering the koan is seen as a means of enlightenment. Pure Soto Zen does not use the koan.

Both Rinzai Zen and Soto Zen use the typical Zen method of meditation—*zazen,* sitting meditation. Detailed instructions for zazen include positioning of the body, including the tongue and teeth. The eyes are kept open, in contrast to many meditation techniques. The goal of zazen is satori, mystical enlightenment.

Since Zen arrived, in 1893, and spread after World War II it has become the most popular form of Buddhism for non-Asiatic Americans, Presently, Zen centers can be found in most American cities, with a few—such as the Zen Meditation Center of Rochester (NY) and the Zen Center of San Francisco—heading up a chain of centers.[7]

SOKA GAKKAI

Soka Gakkai is the popular name for Nichiren Shoshu, originally a lay movement that grew up among the Japanese followers of Nichiren Buddhism. Intensely nationalistic, it was suppressed by the Shinto government but revived after World War II. It went from less than a hundred members to approximately a quarter million.

Soka Gakkai became an object of strong dislike for most Japanese Buddhists and was even alienated from other Nichiren Buddhists, because it entered into politics and developed harsh proselytizing techniques. It organized its own political party, the Komei Kai, which in the 1960s became a major force on the national political scene.

The Nichiren Shoshu also engaged in a practice called shaku-buku, literally translated "bend and flatten." This proselytizing technique reportedly included bullying and badgering families of Soka Gakkai members into also joining and applying undue pressure on the vulnerable. Little evidence of the use of shaku-buku has been manifest in the Nichiren Shoshu of America.

Nichiren (1222-82) taught that salvation came through the teachings of the Lotus Sutra, a Buddhist text he believed represented Buddhism in its most primitive and pure form. Each person can attain enlightenment by being in harmony with the universal law. Happiness and peace is attained by chanting the Daimoku, a mantra-like phrase, "namu myoho renge kyo"—that is, "reverence for the wonderful law of the lotus"—and by reciting the Lotus Sutra. Members recite the sutra and invoke repetitively the Daimoku at least twice daily—morning and evening—before the Gohonzon, an enshrined scroll on which the Daimoku is written. Individuals may also carry a Gohonzon scroll on their person and repeat the Daimoku as they feel led.

After coming to America in the early 1960s, the Nichiren Shoshu experienced a rapid growth among non-Orientals in the late sixties and spread into a national movement in the early seventies. George N. Williams, a Caucasian, became its General Director and led its development so that now units can be found in most major U.S. cities.[8]

CHRISTIAN "CULTS"

In the late 1960s a new revival of traditional Protestant Christianity began among the flower children who had gathered in California. The flower culture had created a new mode of living: "on the street." The street people walked the streets during the day and found any convenient pad to flop on in the evening. Their life evolved around psychedelic drugs, psychedelic art and music, and underground newspapers.

To bring the message of salvation in Jesus to these street people, evangelists moved onto the streets to preach and distribute their Christian underground newspapers. The early activity of people like Duane Petersen and Don Williams sparked a national movement of young adults into conservative Christianity. The converts became known as the Jesus People. The Jesus People movement found quick support among mainline churches, who at first encouraged it and later co-opted and absorbed much of it. Nevertheless, the movement produced several new denominations.

Soon after the movement began, theological conflict developed, and some groups were denounced for their recruitment tactics. At least four groups were accused of irregularities by the main body of Jesus People. These same groups later became the focus of anti-cult activity.

THE CHILDREN OF GOD/THE FAMILY OF LOVE

The Children of God began as a unit of Teen Challenge, the street ministry begun by Pentecostalist David Wilkerson. David Brandt Berg led the Teen Challenge unit in Huntington Beach, California. In 1969 Berg received a revelation that California was threatened by a major earthquake, and as a result, he led his followers on an eight-month trek through the Southwest. The trek, which ended in Texas in 1970, became the constituting event for the group. They saw it as an Exodus-like journey, and Berg, now in place as an independent teacher, began to call himself Moses David.

The Children of God accept the basic framework of traditional Christianity, although deviating at several key points. They accept the writings of Moses David as an authority equal to the Bible. These writings are regularly published in a series of tracts and pamphlets called *Mo Letters*. They are communalists. Although communalism has a long and honored history in the church, after the first generations it was always a minority practice. Communal ideals have been particularly abhorrent to modern anti-cultists.

The Children of God have been most criticized for their sexual teachings. They have been accused of condoning lesbianism, using sex to attract new members, and practicing polygamy (at least in the case of Moses David). There may be some merit to the accusations, but in the heated anti-cult climate no evaluation of the scope of the practices has been possible.

The Children of God spread quickly, aided by the early movement of several prominent Jesus People into their ranks. They were also the first target of the anti-cultist's and deprogrammer Ted Patrick. In 1974 the Attorney General of the State of New York published a report of his investigation and accused them of a variety of crimes. Due partly to pressure put on them in the United States, the Children of God moved many of their members out of the United States to Europe and Latin America. Moses David himself moved first to Puerto Rico and more recently settled in London. World headquarters were moved to Switzerland. As of 1980, less than 500 members remain in the United States. They also recently changed their name to the Family of Love.

THE CHRISTIAN FOUNDATION

The Christian Foundation's work preceded the main phase of the Jesus People revival by several years and was for a while an integral part of it. They were one in doctrine with the mainline of the movement. They differed from much of the mainline by their separatism, their high pressure evangelism, and the strict communal discipline to which members adhered.

Tony and Susan Alamo began the Foundation in 1967. Both had been reared as Jews. To pursue a singing career Tony had changed his name from Bernie Lazar Hoffman. With the help of the Full Gospel Businessmen's Fellowship International, a lay Pentecostal group, the Alamos established their Foundation's headquarters on a ranch near Saugus, California, from where they launched preaching missions into Los Angeles.

People attracted by the Alamos' ministry were invited to spend a weekend at the ranch. Conflict developed when people returned from these weekends and accused the Alamos of keeping them virtual prisoners and badgering them to convert by using highly manipulative techniques.

In the midst of growing criticism the Alamos pulled up stakes and shifted their center of activity to a small town in Arkansas, where they own and operate several businesses. They also opened a Western clothing store in Nashville, Tennessee. In recent years they have toned down their evangelism efforts and kept the Foundation somewhat isolated. As they have moved into a more settled condition, the criticism and controversy have lessened considerably.

THE LOCAL CHURCH

The Local Church (a title given to this group by outsiders) was begun in China by a lay evangelist, Watchman Nee. The movement spread in pre-Maoist China. Nee was arrested by the Communist government in 1952 and spent the last 20 years of his life in prison.

Nee's theology derived from the Plymouth Brethren, whose fundamentalist teaching permeated Protestantism in the late 19th century. The Brethren emphasized dispensationalism, a method of viewing Bible history as a series of different dispensations or periods of God's differing activity in the world. The Brethren opposed denominational Christianity. Nee's particular variation on this ecclesiastical theme gave the group its name. He believed there could be only one true church in any one community. The local church is the gathering of all Christians in a particular area.

Nee has rarely been accused of heresy—at least on any major issue—and his books can be found in Christian bookstores. Possibly the most distinctive doctrinal deviation is their practice of multiple baptisms, which they call "burying." They baptize a member as many times as he or she feels the need to bury the "old man" within. Main criticism of the group comes from other Christians who have accused the Local Church of "sheep-stealing" among their members and of disrupting gatherings of non-Local Church people.

The Local Church has congregations in most cities across North America, but they have kept a low profile. Evangelism is done primarily by word of mouth and few items of their own publications go to nonmembers. Hence, most people rarely hear of their presence. Headquarters are at the Church in Anaheim, California.[9]

WAY INTERNATIONAL

Like the Local Church, the Way International was in existence for many years before the Jesus People revival but for several years was considered an integral part of the revival. Like the Children of God, however, the Way was denounced by the mainstream of the Jesus People movement for its doctrinal distinctiveness, particularly the Way's belief that Jesus is not God, that the dead are not alive until Christ's return, and that every born-again believer can and should manifest all the gifts of the Spirit (mentioned in 1 Corinthians 12).

The Way International was founded in 1942 as the Vesper Chimes, but its name was changed in 1955 to the Way, Inc. and later to the Way International, in 1975. The Way's founder, Victor Paul Wierwille, was at that time a minister of the Evangelical and Reformed Church (now part of the United Church of Christ) but resigned from that body in 1957.

The Way International is organized on the model of a tree, from the Root (international headquarters) to Trunks (national organizations) to Limbs (state and province organizations) to Branches (organizations in cities and towns) to Twigs (small, individual fellowship groups). Individual members are likened to Leaves. New members usually come into the Way through taking the basic 12-session course developed by Wierwille, called "Power for Abundant Living," in which the teachings of the Way are presented. Several options are open to graduates of the course. Many continue to attend Twig fellowships. Others become more involved by attending the Way College, in Emporia, Kansas; by joining the Way Corps; or by becoming a "Way over the World Ambassador" for one year. Each program is designed to give practical application to the Way's biblical teachings.

The Way considers itself to be a biblical research, teaching, and household fellowship ministry. It neither builds nor owns any church buildings but rather meets in home fellowships. Often overlooked by those who write about the Way's development is the role that Wierwille's research in Aramaic has played. He was spurred on by his contact with and personal relationship to Dr. George M. Lamsa, translator of the Lamsa Bible. Among the activities of the Way have been the establishment of a large Aramaic facility (completely computerized) and the training of a group of scholars in the Aramaic (Syrian) language.

Like the Local Church, the Way teaches a form of dispensationalism, although Wierwille prefers the term administration. According to Wierwille, we (present believers) live under the Church administration that began at Pentecost. Scripture from before Pentecost is not addressed to the Church but is for our learning. Pre-Pentecost scripture includes the Old Testament, the Four Gospels, the epistles of Hebrews and James, and Acts (which serves as a transition volume). The Gospels belong to the previous Christ Administration.

Doctrinally, the Way could be considered both Arian and Pentecostal. It rejects the Trinitarian orthodoxy of most of Western Christianity. It believes in the divinity of Jesus, the divine conception of Jesus by God, and that he is the Son of God but not God the Son. It also believes in receiving the fullness of the Holy Spirit, God's power, which may be evidenced by the nine manifestations of the Spirit: speaking in tongues, interpretation of tongues, prophecy, word of knowledge, word of wisdom, discerning of spirits, faith (believing), miracles, and healing.

Criticism of the Way has been mounting and intense. Most has focused on the standard anti-cult theme, accusing the Way of brainwashing and Wierwille of growing rich off the movement. A prime additional criticism claims that Wierwille has been training the Way members in the use of deadly weapons for possible future violent activity against the group's enemies. This criticism derived from the Way College's cooperation with the State of Kansas program to promote hunting safety, in which all students had the choice (but were not required) to enroll. No evidence of any violent motivations, intent, or actions has been produced to back up this harsh criticism.

Headquarters of the Way International are in New Knoxville, Ohio, on the site of the homestead where Dr. Wierwille was born. The Wierwille family donated the farm and lands to the Way International organization, and an expansive center has developed. An annual gathering, the Rock of Ages, is held there and attracts followers in the tens of thousands from both the United States and abroad.

THE UNIFICATION CHURCH

The Unification Church (full name: The Holy Spirit Association for the Unification of World Christianity) is the essence of what constitutes a cult in the mind of popular anti-cultism. From the Unification Church come such terms as heavenly deception and love bombing. While becoming the best-known cult in America, its leader, the Rev. Sun Myung Moon, has become one of the ten most hated men in the land. To understand the controversy that has surrounded the Church it is necessary to look first at its history and beliefs.

The Unification Church was founded in 1954, in Seoul, Korea, by Reverend Moon. Eighteen years earlier he had had a vision of Jesus, who told him that he would have a mission to perform. In subsequent years Moon discovered the Divine Principle from which the teachings of the Church derive. The Church was brought to the United States in 1959 but did not experience significant growth until the 1970s, when Moon began a series of national preaching tours and eventually moved to the United States.

The teachings found literary expression in a book, the *Divine Principle,* which has gone through several editions in an attempt to present the Principle more accurately. The teachings begin in the understanding of creation.*

*The theological teachings of the Unification Church are presented here in some detail, as one accusation against the Church has been that it is

150

The Unification Church teaches that the Infinite God can be known by the study of His Creation. Everything exists in pairs—masculine and feminine, positive and negative, initiative and receptive. God contains the same polarity. All things also contain an inner and outer nature. In like measure, God's Internal Nature (Sung-sang) is His heart of infinite love, and His External Form (Hyung-sang) is the energy of the universe.

God created the universe to bring Himself joy and to bring joy to humanity. All men and women have the capacity to reflect fully the image of God and become one with Him. Oneness is achieved when individuals develop fully their capacity to love. In family life one ideally finds the most complete expression of the range and depth of human love. God's love is the infinite counterpart of the three modes of human love: love of parents for children, love of husband and wife, and love of children for parents.

Because God is the substantial being of goodness and the eternal idea in accordance with His purpose, humans were also created to become ideal embodiments of goodness, in whom sin and suffering would be a contradiction and an impossibility. The reality of the contradictions and evil in which humans find themselves is a result of having lost the original value by falling.

Having fallen into sin, humans must tread the path of salvation under God's blessing; in the Unification Principle, salvation is restoration. In other words, the purpose of salvation is to return to the original state before the fall; therefore, God's providence of salvation is the providence of restoration. In this restoration process, Christ comes as the mediator and the example of how to live spiritually and physically to become God's ideal. Therefore, by uniting the heart and action with Christ, people are "saved."

The teachings postulate that Jesus was supposed to take a bride and create the ideal family, but his early death limited this plan. In essence Jesus fell short of completing his assigned task and the first Advent brought only "spiritual" salvation and a promise to return. The Lord of the Second Advent will bring "physical" salvation. To

not a genuinely religious organization and hence has little or no religious perspective.

church members, the Second Coming is at hand and Reverend Moon is the prophet whose revelation and work are preparing the way.

A spiritual world exists as the counterpart of the physical. In the physical world we as humans mature our spirits within the limits of time so we will be prepared to live with God eternally. Heaven is the highest level of the spiritual world where perfected people dwell in oneness with God.

The Unification Church is organized hierarchically. It is headed by Reverend Moon and an international board of directors. A national president is named for each country and is directly accountable to the board and Reverend Moon. In the United States, state and local leaders are appointed by the president. The national Church also controls the various departments of Church activity. For example, the Church operates a medical mission program in West Africa, which is conducted from the national headquarters in New York City.[10]

APPENDIX B

RESOLUTION ON DEPROGRAMMING
"Religious Liberty for Young People Too"

Adopted by the Governing Board of the National Council of Churches, February 28, 1974.

In this country, kidnapping a young person for ransom is a federal crime of utmost seriousness, but kidnapping such a person in order to change his or her religious beliefs and commitments has not thus far actuated federal authorities to invoke the statute. Grand juries have refused to indict and petit juries to convict persons charged with such acts, apparently because done at the behest of parents or other relatives and ostensibly for the good of the victim.

Sometimes the victim is unarguably a minor, subject to the authority of his or her parents. In other instances, the victim is over 25 or 30, clearly an adult competent to make his or her own commitments in religion as in other matters. The rest are between 18 and 21 years of age, and their claims to adulthood are clouded by the vagaries and variety of federal, state and local laws.

The Governing Board of the NCC believes that religious liberty is one of the most precious rights of humankind, which is grossly violated by forcible abduction and protracted efforts to change a

153

person's religious commitments by duress. Kidnapping for ransom is heinous indeed, but kidnapping to compel religious deconversion is equally criminal. It violates not only the letter and spirit of state and federal statutes, but the world standard of the Universal Declaration of Human Rights, which states: "Everyone has the right to freedom of thought, conscience and religion; this right includes freedom to change his religion or belief, and freedom, either alone or in community with others and in public or private, to manifest his religion or belief in teaching, practice, worship and observance."

The Governing Board is mindful of the intense anguish which can motivate parents at the defection of their offspring from the family faith, but in our view this does not justify forcible abduction. We are aware that religious groups are accused of "capturing" young people by force, drugs, hypnotism, "brainwashing," etc. If true, such actions should be prosecuted under the law, but thus far the evidence all runs the other way: it is the would-be rescuers who are admittedly using force.

The Governing Board recognizes that parents have the ultimate responsibility for the religious nurture of their children until they become adults in their own right, and parents are morally and legally justified in using reasonable force to carry out their responsibility (even if in matters of religion it may be unwise, ineffective or counterproductive). Nevertheless, at some point, young people are entitled to make their own decisions in religion as in other matters. What that point should be may vary from family to family, since emancipation is surely in most cases virtually complete by 18.

The Governing Board has previously urged the right to vote for 18 year-olds* and welcomes the action of those states which are making all rights of citizenship effective at 18 rather than 21. The right to choose and follow one's own religion without forcible interference should likewise be guaranteed at least by that age.

*June 3, 1965. Based on Policy Statement: Approval of Article XIII of the Draft International Covenant of Human Rights—November 28, 1951.

154

NOTES

Introduction

1. P.J. Philip in Foreword to Charles Y. Glock and Robert N. Bellah, eds., *The New Religious Consciousness* (Berkeley: University of California Press, 1976), p. ix.
2. Gini Graham Scott, *Cult and Countercult: A Study of a Spiritual Growth Group and a Witchcraft Order* (Westport, CT.: Greenwood Press, 1980), pp. 11-15.
3. See Jonathan Edwards, *A Treatise Concerning Religious Affections,* published in 1746. A good recent edition, edited by John E. Smith, was published by Yale University Press under the title *Religious Affections* in 1959.
4. *Yearbook of American and Canadian Churches* (Nashville: Abingdon Press).
5. Lewis Lancaster, "Buddhism in the United States," *International Buddhist Forum Quarterly,* introductory issue, September 1977, 26-29.
6. Rodney Stark, William Sims Bainbridge, and Daniel P. Doyle, "Cults of America: A Reconnaissance in Space and Time," *Sociological Analysis,* vol. 40, 1979, 347-59.

Chapter 1 Understanding Cults

1. Cf. Geoffrey K. Nelson, *Spiritualism and Society* (New York: Schocken Books, 1969), pp. 217-37, or more recently, Rodney Stark and William Sims Bainbridge, "Churches, Sects, and Cults," *Journal for the Scientific Study of Religion*, vol. 18, no. 2 (June 1979), 117-31.

2. Early and influential books on cults from an evangelical Christian perspective would include William Irvine's *Timely Warnings*, originally issued in 1917 and kept in print under later titles *Modern Heresies Exposed* and *Heresies Exposed* (New York: Loizeaux Brothers); and Jan Karel Van Baalen, *The Chaos of Cults* (4th ed., rev.; Grand Rapids: William B. Eerdmans, 1962), originally released in 1938.

3. For an overview of each family and each religious group in it, see J. Gordon Melton, *The Encyclopedia of American Religions* (Wilmington, NC: McGrath Publishing Co., 1978).

4. The annual *Yearbook of American and Canadian Churches* (Nashville: Abingdon Press), originally conceived as a directory of the members of the Federal Council of Churches, only lists several hundred of the more established churches and sects. The majority are missed because they will not report or the editor has chosen to exclude them.

5. Cf. Kate Carter, *Denominations That Base Their Beliefs on the Teachings of Joseph Smith* (Salt Lake City: Daughter of the Utah Pioneers, 1969).

6. Cf. Charles S. Braden, *Spirits in Rebellion: The Rise and Development of New Thought* (Dallas: Southern Methodist University Press, 1967).

7. Cf. J. Stillson Judah, *The History and Philosophy of the Metaphysical Movements in America* (Philadelphia: Westminster Press, 1967).

8. Cf. Margot Adler, *Drawing Down the Moon* (New York: Viking Press, 1979).

9. David B. Barrett, *Schism and Renewal in Africa* (Nairobi: Oxford University Press, 1968).

10. Cf. Charles G. Finney, *Revival Lectures* (Old Tappan, NJ: Fleming H. Revell Co., 1968), frequently reprinted. On the development of evangelism and recruitment techniques see, for example, J. Wilbur Chapman, *Revivals and Missions* (New York: Lentilhon, 1900); Jonas Oramel Peck, *The Revival and the Pastor*, 1894); and J.H. MacDonald, *The Revival/A Symposium* (Cincinnati: Jennings and Graham, 1905). For a more modern treatment see E. Griffin, *The Mind Changers* (Wheaton, IL: Tyndale House Pubs., 1976).

11. Carl Oblinger, *Religious Mimesis*, (Evanston, IL: Institute for the Study of American Religion, 1973).

12. Cf. John Henry Barrows, *The World's Parliament of Religions* (Chicago: Parliament Publishing Company, 1893).

13. In reporting membership in alternative religions we have relied on a collection of articles and papers in which an actual survey and count of a group was made. In this way we have avoided the misleading misrepresentations of much anti-cult literature, such as the error-filled volume by Jim Siegelman and Flo Conway, *Snapping* (New York: J.B. Lippincott Co., 1978).

14. J. Gordon Melton, *Neo-Paganism: Report on the Survey of an Alternative Religion*, a paper presented to the Society for the Scientific Study of Religion meeting in Cincinnati, Ohio, October 30-November 2, 1980.

Chapter 2   *Understanding the Cultist: Snapping or Transformation?*

1. See, for example, the popular but misleading book by Jim Siegelman and Flo Conway, *Snapping* (New York: J.B. Lippincott Co., 1978).

2. For an analysis of the human experience of the eruption of the sacred into the ordinary world, see Mircea Eliade, *The Sacred and the Profane: The Nature of Religion*, translated by Willard Trask (New York: Harcourt Brace Jovanovich, 1968).

3. Clinicians often speak of this as the parents' use of the children

as "self-objects," in this case as a means for the parents to bolster their own fragile self-esteem.

4. Professor Richardson's ideas on this topic were shared with a working group on the "new religions" held at a recent meeting of the Society for the Scientific Study of Religion.

5. See the extensive literature from the various perspectives on the psychology of conversion listed in Donald Capps, et al., eds., *Psychology of Religion: A Guide to Information Sources* (Detroit: Gale Research Co., 1976). A careful examination of this bibliography will also help the reader to understand the complexity of issues in this field of study and the necessity to consult specialists before offering generalizations for public consumption. We have also included a number of the most important books on the topic in our selected bibliography.

6. Siegelman and Conway, *Snapping*, op. cit.

7. See Robbins' bibliography on the topic, *Civil Liberties, "Brainwashing" and "Cults"* (Berkeley, CA: Program for the Study of New Religious Movements in America, 1979).

8. See, for example, the report of research by Marc Galanter et al. in "The 'Moonies': A Psychological Study of Conversion and Membership in a Contemporary Religious Sect," *American Journal of Psychiatry*, vol. 136, no. 2 (February 1979), 165-70.

9. We recommend the discussion of personality development and the origins of psychopathology in Gertrude Blanck and Rubin Blanck, *Ego Psychology: Theory and Practice* (New York: Columbia University Press, 1974), and *Ego Psychology II: Psychoanalytic Developmental Psychology* (New York: Columbia University Press, 1979).

10. By far the best recent discussion of these issues may be found in the book by David G. Bromley and Anson D. Shupe Jr., two sociologists who have made an outstanding contribution to rational analysis of the cult experience. Their book *Strange Gods* (Boston: Beacon Press, 1981) is required reading for anyone seeking understanding of this phenomenon.

11. Daniel J. Levinson, *The Seasons of a Man's Life* (New York: Alfred A. Knopf, 1978).

12. A good introduction is his *The Ritual Process: Structure and Anti-Structure* (Ithaca, NY: Cornell University Press, 1977). Robert S. Ellwood Jr. has pioneered in emphasizing to us the importance of Turner's work for understanding minority religions. See Ellwood's excellent *Alternative Altars: Unconventional and Eastern Spirituality in America* (Chicago: University of Chicago Press, 1979), pp. 28-32. Figure 2 is adapted from *The Ritual Process*, pp. 106-7.

13. See also Turner's essay, "Betwixt and Between: The Liminal Period in Rites of Passage" in his *The Forest of Symbols* (Ithaca,NY: Cornell University Press, 1967), pp. 93-111.

14. Arnold van Gennep, *Rites of Passage*, translated by Monika Vizedon and Gabrielle L. Caffee (Chicago: University of Chicago Press, 1960).

15. A helpful glossary of Turner's technical terms may be found in the appendix of Victor Turner and Edith Turner, *Image and Pilgrimage in Christian Culture: Anthropological Perspectives* (New York: Columbia University Press, 1978), pp. 243-55.

16. Turner, *The Ritual Process*, op. cit., p. 96.

17. Ibid., p. 95.

18. Ibid.

19. Erich Lindemann, "Symptomatology and Management of Acute Grief," *American Journal of Psychiatry*, vol. 101, 1944, 141-51. For a solid review of the literature and application to counseling situations, see David K. Switzer, *The Dynamics of Grief* (Nashville: Abingdon Press, 1970).

20. Granger E. Westberg, *Minister and Doctor Meet* (New York: Harper & Row, 1961), p. 99. Copyright © 1961 by Granger E. Westberg. Reprinted by permission of Harper & Row, Publishers, Inc.

21. Ibid.

22. Ibid.

23. Cf. the discussion of therapeutic relationships in Jerome Frank's classic book on the subject, *Persuasion and Healing: A Comparative Study of Psychotherapy* (rev. ed.; New York: Schocken Books, 1974).

24. Margaret T. Singer, "Coming Out of the Cults," *Psychology Today*, vol. 12, no. 8, pp. 72-82.
25. Ibid., p. 75
26. Examine, for example, the treatment by Anson D. Shupe Jr. and David G. Bromley in *The New Vigilantes* (Beverly Hills, CA: Sage Press, 1980).
27. See the discussion of regression in service of the ego in Ernst Kris, *Psychoanalytic Explorations in Art* (New York: International Universities Press, 1952).
28. Compare the case of John Wesley and the early Methodist movement as discussed in Robert L. Moore, *John Wesley and Authority: A Psychological Perspective* (Missoula, MT: Scholars Press, 1979).
29. Here again we recommend that the reader consult the discussion of these issues by Gertrude Blanck and Rubin Blanck in their books referred to above in note 9.
30. For a solid introduction to the family systems perspective see the chapter on family therapy in Raymond Corsini, ed., *Current Psychotherapies* (2d ed.; Itasca, IL: F.E. Peacock, 1979).
31. See, for example, Joan E. Farley, "Family Separation-Individuation Tolerance—A Developmental Conceptualization of the Nuclear Family," *Journal of Marital and Family Therapy*, vol. 5, no. 1 (January 1979), 61-67; and Sally Hughes, Michael Berger, and Larry Wright, "The Family Life Cycle and Clinical Intervention," *Journal of Marriage and Family Counseling*, vol. 4, no. 4 (October 1978), 33-39.

Chapter 3   Deprogramming and the Anti-cult Movement

1. The literature on cults and deprogramming is quite large. For a sample listing see Tom Robbins' *Civil Liberties, "Brainwashing" and "Cults"* (Berkeley, CA: Program for the Study of New Religious Movements in America, 1979). The recent book edited by John Garvey, *All Our Sons and Daughters* (Springfield,

IL: Templegate Publishers, 1977), includes chapters by exponents from the wide range of opinions.

2. Joel A. MacCollam, *Carnival of Souls: Religious Cults and Young People* (New York: Seabury Press, 1979), p. 119.

3. Christopher Edwards, *Crazy for God* (Englewood Cliffs, NJ: Prentice-Hall, 1979).

4. Kent Levitt, *Kidnapped for My Faith* (Van Nuys, CA: Bible Voice, 1978).

5. Account included in Ted Patrick and Tom Dulack, *Let Our Children Go* (New York: E.P. Dutton, 1976).

6. Barbara Underwood and Betty Underwood, *Hostage to Heaven* (New York: Clarkson N. Potter, Inc., 1979).

7. The Institute for the Study of American Religion (ISAR) files contain an affidavit by Arthur Roselle and a set of affidavits by Wendy Helander that tell her story. For Helander's parents' account see Barbara Grizzuti Harrison, "The Struggle for Wendy Helander," *McCall's*, October 1979, pp. 87-94.

8. Patrick and Dulack, *Let Our Children Go*, op. cit., p. 15.

9. Ibid., p. 75.

10. Jim Siegelman and Flo Conway, *Snapping* (New York: J.B. Lippincott Co., 1978) .

11. Patrick and Dulack, *Let Our Children Go*, op. cit., p. 21.

12. "Playboy Interview with Ted Patrick," *Playboy*, March 1979, pp. 53-58, 60-88, 220. Originally appeared in PLAYBOY magazine. Copyright © 1978 by Playboy.

13. Patrick and Dulack, *Let Our Children Go*, op. cit., p. 24.

14. Levitt, *Kidnapped for My Faith*, op. cit., p. 37.

15. Ibid., p. 36.

16. "Playboy Interview," op. cit.

17. Roselle affidavit.

18. A copy of Taylor's affidavit is in the files of the ISAR.

19. Patrick and Dulack, *Let Our Children Go*, op. cit., p. 78.

20. Underwood and Underwood, *Hostage to Heaven*, op. cit., p. 235.

21. Edwards, *Crazy for God*, op. cit., p 207.

22. "Playboy Interview," op. cit.

23. Patrick and Dulack, *Let Our Children Go*, op. cit., p. 35.

24. "Playboy Interview" op. cit.
25. Rachel Martin, *Escape* (Denver: Accent Books, 1979).
26. Charles Remberg and Bonnie Remberg, "The Rescue of Alison Cardais," *Good Housekeeping*, April 1976, pp. 108-09, 134, 138, 140-41.
27. Such alternatives are available in the standard techniques developed in family counseling (to be discussed below). See also "Mediation as an Alternative to Deprogramming," a leaflet being distributed by the Berkeley Area Interfaith Council, 2340 Durant Avenue, Berkeley, CA 94704
28. The story of the development and actions of the national deprogramming movement has been ably documented and told by Anson D. Shupe Jr. and David G. Bromley in *The New Vigilantes* (Beverly Hills, CA: Sage Publications, 1980). The account in this section has been drawn from *The New Vigilantes* supplemented by the authors.

Chapter 4 Responding to the New Religious Pluralism: An Agenda for Action

1. Ernest Becker, *Escape from Evil* (New York: The Free Press, 1975). See also his Pulitzer prize-winning book, *The Denial of Death* (New York: The Free Press, 1973).
2. Erich Neumann, *Depth Psychology and a New Ethic* (New York: C.G. Jung Foundation Publications, 1969).
3. Personal communication to Robert Moore, October 30, 1981.
4. Conservative Christians have recently been offering their criticisms of secular humanism from the point of view of evangelical theology. Our concern here is rather to emphasize the complexity of religious phenomena, such as conversion, and the extent of study necessary even to understand the current state of research on the topic. The hermeneutical problems involved are extremely complex and require considerable philosophical sophistication.
5. This is, of course, what Jungian psychologists term the projec-

tion of the "shadow," or denied aspects of one's own personality.

6. We are using the word object here in a manner informed by psychoanalytic ego psychology in general and object relations theory in particular. See, for example, Otto F. Kernberg, *Object Relations Theory and Its Applications* (New York: Jason Aronson, Inc., 1977). The concept of splitting as understood in object relations theory is another way to talk about the psychodynamics behind the phenomenon of scapegoating. Indeed, the need to portray members of the alternative religions in stereotyped, dehumanizing caricatures would be grounded in the object relations of the *interpreter,* not those of the persons so interpreted.

7. One who has not become culturally "modern" usually uses more traditional and less subtle grounds for his or her depreciation of the alien other. The modern secularist with scientific pretensions seeks to justify shadow projections with charts and statistics.

8. Jim Siegelman and Flo Conway continue to make pronouncements on religious phenomena that sound scientific to a lay person but which are vastly oversimplified and misleading. See their recent article, "Information Disease: Have Cults Created a New Mental Illness?" in *Science Digest,* January 1982, 86-92. Here again we note the prestige of science being placed in the service of the anti-cult movement. Compare this article with the treatment of similar issues by David G. Bromley and Anson D. Shupe Jr. in their book *Strange Gods* (Boston: Beacon Press, 1981). *Strange Gods* is an excellent survey from a sociological point of view and should be read alongside this volume as an elaboration of the approach we recommend.

9. We recommend, for example, an examination of Paul Ricoeur's work on the philosophical and linguistic problems involved in such interpretations. See his *Freud and Philosophy* (New Haven: Yale University Press, 1970) and his *Hermeneutics and the Human Sciences: Essays on Language, Action, and Interpretation,* edited by John B. Thompson (New York: Cambridge University Press, 1981). We also find among many popular

psychological interpreters of the alternative religions an inexcusable lack of familiarity with the scholarly literature of the psychology of religion. For an introduction to this important body of scholarship see Donald Capps, et al., eds., *Psychology of Religion: A Guide to Information Sources* (Detroit: Gale Research Co., 1976).

10. For provocative discussions of this increasing "religious" role of psychology see Philip Rieff, *The Triumph of the Therapeutic: Uses of Faith After Freud* (New York: Harper & Row, 1968), and Paul C. Vitz, *Psychology as Religion: The Cult of Self-Worship* (Grand Rapids: William B. Eerdmans, 1977).

11. It is easy to see the financial interest that may influence the interpretations of deprogrammers and others who may wish to sell their services to distraught parents.

12. See the discussions of the field of religious studies in American colleges and universities in Clyde A. Holbrook, *Religion: A Humanistic Field* (Westport, CT: Greenwood Press, 1978); Paul Ramsey, ed., *Religion* (Englewood Cliffs, NJ: Prentice-Hall, 1965); Claude Welsh, *Graduate Education in Religion: A Critical Appraisal* (Missoula, MT: University of Montana Press, 1971); and Council on Graduate Studies in Religion, *A Guide to the Programs of the Council on Graduate Studies in Religion* (The Council, 1979).

13. Specialists in religious studies have already been providing significant contributions toward understanding minority religions. The work of Robert S. Ellwood Jr., for example, has been very important. See his *Religious and Spiritual Groups in Modern America* (Englewood Cliffs, NJ: Prentice-Hall, 1973), and his *Alternative Altars: Unconventional and Eastern Spirituality in America* (Chicago: University of Chicago Press, 1979). For his overview of research in this area see his article "The Study of New Religious Movements in America," Council on the Study of Religion *Bulletin,* vol. 10, no. 3 (June 1979), 69-72. For an excellent introduction to the history and phenomenology of religion see Frederick J. Streng, *Understanding Religious Life* (2d ed.; Belmont, CA: Dickenson Publishing Co., 1976).

14. Prof. Walter Capps, of the University of California at Santa

Barbara, recently provided an argument for an increased public leadership role for religious scholars in his article "Contemporary Socio-Political Change and the Work of Religious Studies," Council on the Study of Religion *Bulletin,* vol. 12, no. 4 (October 1981), 93-95.

15. All too often legislative bodies have not sought out the help of the American Academy of Religion in gathering information for interpreting religious phenomena in the context of the cult experience. In the future we as citizens must insist that such bodies seek out expert testimony from competent religious scholars.

16. Already a significant number of clergy are pursuing such studies in religious studies programs around the country. This is a trend that should be encouraged as part of continuing education programs for clergy.

17. For an introduction to this topic see Kenneth Leech, *Soul Friend: The Practice of Christian Spirituality* (New York: Harper & Row, 1980). See also Urban T. Holmes III, *Ministry and Imagination* (New York: Seabury Press, 1976).

18. Many lay members of mainline congregations find that their local churches do not provide them with a context in which careful examination of their lives as religious pilgrimages may be made. We as church leaders tend to be more comfortable if parishioners present their concerns to us in the language of psychological distress. Instead of having to face our responsibilities as spiritual directors we can then do what the "competent" professional minister does: Refer the person to the "secular priest," the psychotherapist.

19. See Charles E. Winquist, *Homecoming: Interpretation, Transformation, and Individuation* (Chico, CA: Scholars Press, 1978), and his *Practical Hermeneutics: A Revised Agenda for the Ministry* (Chico, CA: Scholars Press, 1980).

20. Matthew Fox, introduction to *Breakthrough: Meister Eckhart's Creation Spirituality* (New York: Doubleday, 1980).

21. Cf. Erik Erikson, *Identity and the Life Cycle* (New York: International Universities Press, 1959).

22. The American Association of Pastoral Counselors (AAPC) has

long sought to provide the denominations with leadership in mental health-related ministries. Highly trained members of the AAPC work in churches and counseling centers across the country. A list of accredited members and centers can be obtained by writing the Executive Director, American Association of Pastoral Counselors, 9508-A Lee Highway, Fairfax, VA 22031, or by phoning (703) 385-6967.

23. We have reference here to the recent defeat of the Lasher Bill in New York State.

24. Some psychiatrists, for example, have met with parents and group members in neutral settings to facilitate communication and possible reconciliation. We should seek to foster such attempts at mediation across the country. A good model is that of the Berkeley Area Interfaith Council. See the discussion of their work in the pamphlet "Dealing with Someone Who Has Joined a Religious 'Cult': A Guide for Family and Friends," published by Americans Preserving Religious Liberty, San Francisco Bay Area Chapter, 436 14th Street, Suite 1217, Oakland, CA 94612.

25. Our point of view here is similar to that of psychiatrist and family therapist Clara Livsey, who has emphasized the necessity for educating parents in order to reduce the role of family dynamics in pushing young persons into group memberships. See her book *The Manson Women* (New York: Richard Marek Publishers, 1980).

26. See the "Resolution on Deprogramming," adopted by the Governing Board of the National Council of Churches, February 28, 1974. The text of this resolution is reproduced in Appendix B.

Appendix A   A Brief Guide to the Major Alternative Religions

1. For a general survey of alternative religions in America see J. Gordon Melton, *The Encyclopedia of American Religions* (Wil-

mington, NC: McGrath Publishing Co. 1978). It provides the only comprehensive guide to religious bodies currently functioning in the United States. It may be ordered from the Institute for the Study of American Religion, Box 1311, Evanston, IL 60201.
2. *What Is Scientology?* (Los Angeles: Church of Scientology of California, 1978).
3. Margot Adler, *Drawing Down the Moon* (New York: Viking Press, 1979).
4. J. Stillson Judah, *Hare Krishna and the Counterculture* (New York: John Wiley & Sons, 1974).
5. John White, *Everything You Want to Know About TM Including How to Do It* (New York: Pocket Books, 1976).
6. James V. Downton Jr., *Sacred Journeys* (New York: Columbia University Press, 1979).
7. Rick Fields, *How the Swans Came to the Lake* (Boulder, CO: Shambhala, 1981).
8. Kiyoaki Murata, *Japan's New Buddhism* (New York: Walker/ Westherhill, 1969).
9. Angus I. Kinnear, *Against the Tide* (Harrisburg, PA: Christian Literature Crusade, 1973).
10. David G. Bromley and Anson D. Shupe Jr., *"Moonies" in America* (Beverly Hills, CA: Sage Publications, 1979).

SELECTED BIBLIOGRAPHY

General Surveys

At present only two books offer a survey of the 500 to 600 alternative religions presently operating in the United States:

Melton, J. Gordon. *A Directory of Religious Bodies in the United States*. New York: Garland, 1977; 305 pp. Gives names and addresses of over 1,200 religions, including approximately 800 Christian denominations.

———. *The Encyclopedia of American Religions*. Wilmington, NC: McGrath Publishing Co., 1978. See vol. II.

New and Alternative Religions

During the 1970s alternative religions received a great deal of attention from both religious scholars and sociologists, and a large body of material has been gathered that offers a perspective on them. Among the most important items are:

Ellwood, Robert S. Jr. *Alternative Altars: Unconventional and Eastern Spirituality in America*. Chicago: University of Chicago Press, 1979; 192 pp.

———. *Religious and Spiritual Groups in Modern America*. Englewood Cliffs, NJ: Prentice-Hall, 1973; 334 pp.

Gaustad, Edwin Scott. *Dissent in American Religion*. Chicago: University of Chicago Press, 1973; 184 pp. Gives a historical perspective on the role of dissent in American religion.

Glock, Charles Y., and Robert N. Bellah. *The New Religious Consciousness*. Berkeley, CA: University of California Press, 1976; 391 pp.

Needleman, Jacob, and George Baker. *Understanding the New Religions*. New York: Seabury Press, 1978; 314 pp.

Wallis, Roy. *Sectarianism*. London: Owen, 1975; 212 pp. Based primarily on British and Canadian research.

Wuthnow, Robert. *The Consciousness Reformation*. Berkeley, CA: University of California Press, 1978; 221 pp.

———. *Experimentation in American Religion*. Berkeley, CA: University of California Press, 1978; 221 pp.

Zaretsky, Irving I., and Mark P. Leone. *Religious Movements in Contemporary America*. Princeton, NJ: Princeton University Press, 1974; 837 pp.

Withnow's volumes represent the final books to come out of the Danforth project. Zaretsky and Leone bring together a mass of material from all the social sciences.

The Cult Wars

During the 1970s a strong anti-cult movement developed against many of the alternative religions. The "war" on the cults has been fought out in deprogramming attempts, the courts and various legal forums. The following material offers some perspective on and criticism of this movement.

Bromley, David G. and Anson D. Shupe Jr. *Strange Gods*. Boston: Beacon Press, 1981. An appraisal of the cult scare, as these two sociologists term the cult wars of the 1970s; includes recommendations for action or, as in the case of legislation, nonaction. An important contribution that should receive widespread attention.

Garvey, John, ed. *All Our Sons and Daughters*. Springfield, IL: Templegate Publishers, 1977; 131 pp. Almost the only volume to combine essays by people on both sides of the cult war. May be ordered from the publisher at 302 East Adams Street, Springfield, IL 62701; paperback, $3.95.

Richardson, Herbert. *New Religions and Mental Health*. New York: Edwin Mellon Press, 1980; 177 pp. A good collection of articles dealing with the various questions concerning the possible mental damage suffered by members of alternative religions. Includes articles on Jewish issues and a section on conversion.

Robbins, Thomas. *Civil Liberties, "Brainwashing" and "Cults."* Berkeley, CA: Program for the Study of New Religious Movements in America, 1979; 33 pp. Rev. ed., 1981; 48 pp. A lengthy annotated bibliography.

Rubenstein, I.H. *Law on Cults*. Chicago: The Ordain Press, 1981; 120 pp. A fine survey of the legal issues and laws concerning alternative religions. Privately published and may be ordered from the author at Box 68, Chicago, IL 60690; paperback, $4.95.

Shupe, Anson D. Jr. and David G. Bromley. *The New Vigilantes*. Beverly Hills, CA: Sage Press, 1980; 267 pp. Two sociologists report on an almost decade-long study of anti-cultists and their role in religious conflict.

Anti-cult Books

With the exception of the volume of Stoner and Parke, the majority of books on the subject of cults—that is, books written with a hostile perspective on the new and alternative religions—show little knowledge of the groups they discuss and almost no contact with the groups about which they tend to speak so authoritatively. As a whole, they are shallow and full of errors. A few of the more prominent ones are listed here, but they must be read with a realization that they are highly inaccurate about individual groups and the alternative religions in general.

Siegelman, Jim, and Flo Conway. *Snapping*. Philadelphia: J.B. Lippincott Co., 1978; 254 pp. One of the most popular yet one of the most error-filled volumes. The authors are uncritical in their use of accounts by former cultists as information sources. They also included numerous bits of mistaken data apparently without checking source or accuracy.

Hunt, Dave. *The Cult Explosion*. Irvine, CA: Harvest House Publishers, 1980; 270 pp.

Irving, William C. *Heresies Exposed*. New York: Loizeaux Brothers, 1921; 225 pp. The original anti-cult book, and it is still in print.

MacCollam, Joel A. *The Weekend That Never Ends*. New York: Seabury Professional Services, 1977; 37 pp. Expanded ed. as *Carnival of Souls*. New York: Seabury Press, 1977; 188 pp.

Martin, Walter. *The New Cults*. Santa Ana, CA: Vision House, 1980; 419 pp.

Patrick, Ted, and Tom Dulack. *Let Our Children Go*. New York: E.P. Dutton, 1976; 285 pp. Currently under a court order to desist from "kidnapping" activity, Patrick is the original "deprogrammer." His book, now largely obsolete and a frank embarrassment to many anti-cultists, is included here for historical purposes.

Stoner, Carrol, and Jo Anne Parke. *All God's Children*. Radnor, PA: Chilton Book Company, 1977; 324 pp.

Whalen, William. *Strange Gods*. Huntington, IN: Our Sunday Visitor, 1981; 130 pp. The latest book by popular Roman Catholic journalist and anti-cultist.

Most anti-cult books speak from a conservative, evangelical

Christian perspective and concentrate on the ways the author perceives the cult's deviation from his or her particular brand of faith. Concentration is on reasons for disliking the group rather than understanding it, and the picture is highly distorted. Also anti-cult authors tend to rely on one another for information rather than doing primary research; hence, they repeat the errors of their predecessors and the deliberate misrepresentations that have been fostered by some anti-cult organizations.

The major source of primary data to appear in anti-cult books comes from the reports of ex-members who have broken with the group because of an intense internal dispute or deprogramming. Unfortunately, their testimonies are usually highly distorted by their hostility and desire to hurt the group at all costs. For a more balanced approach by an ex-member see:

Martin, Rachel. *Escape*. Denver: Accent Books, 1979; 191 pp. Martin describes the complex process of thought that led her to join the group she affiliated with, the continued questioning of her commitment, and the doubts that led her to break with the group in the end. *Escape* shows the intense thought process, i.e., the rationality, that persists even in the most dedicated "cultist."

Material from a Jewish Perspective

The following materials speak from several Jewish perspectives:

Daum, Annette. *Missionary and Cult Movements*. New York: Department of Interreligious Affairs/Union of American Hebrew Congregations, 1979. A study course for use in religious schools, this volume deals with a major concern of religious groups targeting the Jewish community for proselytization attempts. It carries many of the weaknesses of the anti-cult literature, having been authored by someone who has no firsthand knowledge of the topic. The chapters on the various groups, only four of which are dealt with, consist on the whole of a list of rumors and charges, many of which have subsequently been shown to have no basis in fact. This volume must be used with extreme care.

Haramgaal, Ya'agov. "Deprogramming: A Critical View," *The American Zionist*, May-June 1977, pp. 16-19.

Levitt, Kent, with Ceil Rosen. *Kidnapped for My Faith*. Van Nuys, CA: Bible Voice, 1978; 127 pp. Account of a member of the "Jews for Jesus" who was deprogrammed unsuccessfully by his family.

Rudin, James, and Marcia Rudin. *Prison or Paradise/The New Religious Cults*. Philadelphia: Fortress Press, 1980.

Additional Resources

Center for the Study of New Religious Movements, Graduate Theological Union, 2451 Ridge Road, Berkeley, CA 94709

Institute for the Study of American Religion, Box 1311, Evanston, IL 60201, (312) 271-3419.

INDEX

175

176

F

Family of Love, 145-46
Farrow, Mia, 140
Finney, Charles G., 5, 23-24, 32
Fonda, Jane, 140
Food and Drug Administration, 133
Fox, Matthew, 106
Free Minds, Inc., 72
Free Primitive Church of Divine Communion, 21
FREECOG (Free Our Children from the Children of God), 72, 85
Freedom of Thought Foundation, 88
Freud, Sigmund, 70
Full Gospel Businessmen's Fellowship International, 146

G

Gantry, Elmer, 61
Gardner, Gerald, 135
Gohanzon, 144
Graduate Theological Union, 3
Graham, Billy, 32
Great I AM, 130
Greek Orthodox, 86
Grief process, 51-53
Gurus, 60, 137-44
Gutman, Jeremiah, 97

H

Hare Krishna, 15, 26, 37, 81, 90, 125-28, 138-40
Hasidism, 7, 20, 86
Hatha yoga, 27, 137
Hearst, Patty, 81
Helander, Wendy, 73, 81, 88
Hinduism, 7, 9, 18, 25, 27, 101, 104, 120, 137-44
Hoffman, Bernie Lazar, 146

Holiness Movement, 24
Holmes, Urban, 105
Holy Order of MANS, 21
Holy Spirit Association for the Unification of World Christianity, 150
Hubbard, L. Ron, 132

I

Individuation, 63
Institute for the Study of American Religion, 174
Internal Revenue Service, 133
International Foundation for Individual Freedom, 72, 83
International Meditation Society, 140
International Society for Krishna Consciousness, 37, 126, 138-40
Islam, 7, 18, 25

J

Jainism, 7, 25
Jehovah's Witnesses, 26, 87
Jesus People, 145
Jewish Participation in Alternative Religions, 30, 96-97
Jim Roberts' group, 82
Johnson, Lyndon B. (President), 9, 26
Jones, Franklin, 21
Jonestown, Guyana, 16, 89
Judaism, 7, 40, 101

K

Khomeini, Ayatollah, 21
King, Godfre Ray, 130-31
Kirtan, 139
Koan, 143
Krishna, 139

177

Prophet, Elizabeth Clare, 130-31
Prophet, Mark, 130

Q

Quimby, Phineas Parkhurst, 19

R

Radhasoami Satsang Beas, 141-42
Rambur, William, 85
Reformed Churches, 25
Richardson, James, 40
Rinzai Zen, 143
Robbins, Thomas, 41
Roman Catholics, 17-18, 26, 40,
   61, 83, 86, 91
Roselle, Arthur, 73, 76
Rudrananda, Swami, 21
Ruhani Satsang, 21

S

Sanctuary of the Master's
   Presence, 130
Satanism, 126, 134-37
Satguru, 142
Scharff, Gary, 74, 82
Scientology (Scientologists), 15,
   21, 26-27, 132-34
Second Great Awakening, 23
Shin Buddhism, 26
Shinto, 7
Shree Gurudev Rudrananda Yoga
   Ashram, 21
Siddha Yoga Dham, 21
Siegalman, Jim, 86
Sikhism, 12
Singer, Margaret, 56-57
Sivananda Yoga Society, 81
Slaughter, Cynthia, 83
Smith, Joseph, 6, 19
Soka Gakkai, 143-44
Soto Zen, 143

Spiritual Regeneration Movement,
   140
Spiritualism, 11, 17, 19, 21, 24-
   25, 129-30
Stark, Rodney, 11
Sufism, 20
Summit Lighthouse, 130
Symbionese Liberation Army, 81
Synagogue Council of America, 91

T

Taoism, 101
Taylor, Walter, 77
Teen Challenge, 145
Theosophy, 12, 17, 25, 129-30
Thetan, 133
Transcendental Meditation, 5, 27,
   126, 140-41
Turner, Victor, 47, 49-50, 52-53,
   62
Twitchell, Paul, 21

U

Underwood, Barbara, 73-74, 78,
   82
Unification Church, 8, 24, 26-27,
   37, 69, 74, 78, 81, 83, 88,
   90, 125-26, 138, 150-52
Unification Theological Seminary,
   81
Union of American Hebrew
   Congregations, 96
Unitarian Universalist Church, 91
United Church of Christ, 91
United Methodist Church, 91
United Presbyterian Church, 91
United Society, 127
Universal Declaration of Human
   Rights, 91
University of Chicago Divinity
   School, 81